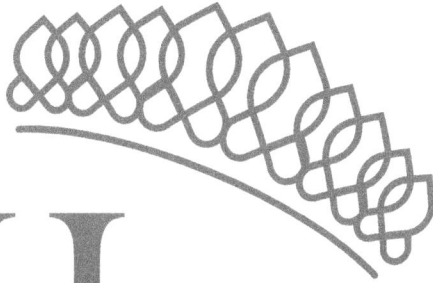

His
BUSINESS

stephanie d. moore

Edited by
Debra M. Smith

Published by
Moore Marketing and Communications, LLC

Oklahoma City, OK
StephanieDMoore.com
MooretoRead.com

Bulk copies or group sales of this book are available by contacting Stephanie D. Moore at moore@stephaniedmoore.com or (405) 306-9833.

Moore, Stephanie D.
His Business
A 31-Day Devotional

Edited by Debra M. Smith

First Edition Printed July 2023
Printed in the USA.

Cover Design and Layout Design by
Moore Marketing and Communications, LLC.
All Rights Reserved.

Cover Photo used in design retrieved on July 8, 2023 at pexels.com, taken by Ketut Subiyanto.

ISBN: 978-1-955544-36-8

I have called you friends,
for everything that I learned from my Father
I have made known to you.

John 15:15

HIS BUSINESS

A 31-Day Devotional

In Loving Memory

Bertha Bradley

*Let us not love
with words or speech
but with actions and in truth.*

I John 3:18

Introduction

There is no greater honor than to be loved and befriended by God. He desires to become friends with each of us, he longs for us to receive his love and to understand his goodwill for every person.

*"As the Father has loved me, so have I loved you.
Now remain in my love.*

If you keep my commands, you will remain in my love, just as I have kept my Father's commands and remain in his love.

I have told you this so that my joy may be in you and that your joy may be complete. My command is this: Love each other as I have loved you.

Greater love has no one than this: to lay down one's life for one's friends. You are my friends if you do what I command.

I no longer call you servants, because a servant does not know his master's business. Instead, I have called you friends, for everything that I learned from my Father I have made known to you.

You did not choose me, but I chose you and appointed you so that you might go and bear fruit—fruit that will last—and so that whatever you ask in my name the Father will give you.

This is my command: Love each other."

John 15:9-17

Friendship with God gives us access to God's plans. In order to receive access, God must trust us and that trust begins in our hearts.

If we love God with all that we are, we are willing to sacrifice that others can experience God's love. We commune with him and spend time with him, so that we may hear his instruction. We not only obey his commands, but we enjoy operating in the will of God. Finally, we see others as God sees them.

We recognize when others are in need. We forgive those who make mistakes just as God forgave us. We sacrifice our comfort so that others may experience comfort. We love others in the same way we want to be loved.

When we are walking with God, spending time with him and doing his will, we are his friends and gain access to the work he is accomplishing on the earth.

To receive the gift of salvation that leads to eternal life, we must only confess and believe in our hearts that Christ died for us. But to gain access to an abundant life, filled with wisdom, stature, and honor, we must place God first and be about His business.

Most Gracious and Heavenly Father,

How precious are Your thoughts toward us, O God! How vast is the sum of them! (1) Every good gift and every perfect gift are from above, coming down from the Father of lights with whom there is no variation or shadow due to change. (2) Therefore, we are thankful in all circumstances, for this is God's will for us who belong to Christ Jesus. (3) Just as we received Christ Jesus as Lord, we continue to live in him, strengthened in the faith as we were taught, and overflowing with thankfulness. (4) We trust in the LORD with all our hearts, and do not lean on our own understanding. In all our ways we acknowledge him, and he will make straight our paths. (5) We will not be conformed to this world, but be transformed by the renewal of our minds, that by testing we may discern what is the will of God, what is good and acceptable and perfect. (6) And it is our prayer that our love may abound more and more, with knowledge and all discernment, so that we may approve what is excellent, and so be pure and blameless for the day of Christ. (7)

The Spirit of the Lord will rest on us—the Spirit of wisdom and of understanding, the Spirit of counsel and of might, the Spirit of the knowledge and fear of the Lord—and we will delight in the fear of the Lord. (8)

In Jesus Name,
Amen

1

GLORY TO HIS NAME

And Jesus increased in wisdom and stature,
and in favor with God and man.
Luke 2:52

Jesus Christ was born to bring glory to His name. In doing so, Jesus shined a light on the love of God for all mankind. When man fell in the garden through the deception of Satan, everything that God taught man was tainted by doubt. Doubt is an indication of unbelief.

The cornerstone of wisdom requires the application of knowledge. Knowledge requires that you trust the information provided. Without receiving necessary information, there is no knowledge, and therefore no wisdom. In order to trust God, you must first know him. In order to know him, you must spend time with him to receive information from him. In order to bring glory to his name, you must exercise wisdom which is the application of knowledge.

Through the application of knowledge (use of wisdom), man gains stature and favor with God and man.

Jesus, born to Mary and Joseph, while in Bethlehem, paying their taxes received confirmation and revelation of Jesus' anointing as the Savior sent by God. This revelation came through the angels that prophesied prior to the birth of Jesus, the shepherds that visited them when he was born, Simeon a just and devout Israelite that was waiting on the birth of Christ, and Anna, a prophet, widow and consistent servant of God through prayer and fasting. The former witnesses were present in the temple when the couple presented Jesus to the church, as accustomed to

Jewish law, 40 days after his birth.

Jesus while still a young boy, at age 12, realized his anointing and began to walk according to all that God instructed.

When his parents honored the tradition of worshipping during the Passover, Jesus was in the synagogues communing with other saints, teaching and sharing his knowledge with them. The people were astounded by how much he knew. Jesus, solely focused on his purpose, which was to bring glory to His name, was busy exercising wisdom. So much so, that when his parents left Jerusalem, they did not realize that Jesus was not with them. Struck with fear, they returned and searched for him. They found him in the temple conversing with doctors, who were listening to Jesus in awe.

His parents asked him why he behaved in such a way, leaving without warning and being found in the temple. Jesus responded that his responsibility was to be about his father's business.

We live in a world that does not consider the business of God, but as servants of the Most High, it is our responsibility to be about the business of God, and that should come before any other business. This can only be accomplished as we allow the Spirit of God to find rest in us, through our consistent worship, praise, and obedience to God. It is not because God is greedy, but because he desires that all of mankind recognize his abundant love, mercy, and grace. We are ambassadors of Christ, our actions matter. Through our obedience, many can meet God, and find rest for their souls.

To receive the gift of salvation that leads to eternal life, we must only confess and believe in our hearts that Christ died for us. But to gain access to an abundant life, filled with wisdom, stature and honor, we must place God first and be about His business.

Most Gracious and Heavenly Father,

How precious are Your thoughts toward us, O God! How vast is the sum of them! (1) Every good gift and every perfect gift is from above, coming down from the Father of lights with whom there is no variation or shadow due to change. (2) Therefore, we are thankful in all circumstances, for this is God's will for us who belong to Christ Jesus. (3) Just as we received Christ Jesus as Lord, we continue to live in him, strengthened in the faith as we were taught, and overflowing with thankfulness. (4) We trust in the LORD with all our hearts, and do not lean on our own understanding. In all our ways acknowledge him, and he will make straight our paths. (5) We will not be conformed to this world, but be transformed by the renewal of our minds, that by testing we may discern what is the will of God, what is good and acceptable and perfect. (6) And it is our prayer that our love may abound more and more, with knowledge and all discernment, so that we may approve what is excellent, and so be pure and blameless for the day of Christ. (7)

The Spirit of the Lord will rest on us—the Spirit of wisdom and of understanding, the Spirit of counsel and of might, the Spirit of the knowledge and fear of the Lord—and we will delight in the fear of the Lord. (8)

Oh, the depth of the riches of the wisdom and knowledge of God! How unsearchable his judgments, and his paths beyond tracing out! Who has known the mind of the Lord? Or who has been his counselor? Who has ever given to God, that God should repay them? For from him and through him and for him are all things. To him be the glory forever! (9)

In Jesus Name,
Amen

2

PREPARED

For we are his workmanship, created in Christ Jesus for good works,
which God prepared beforehand, that we should walk in them.

Ephesians 2:10

God desires that we live in unity with those around us. Our differences are what make us unique, but they should not be a justification for separation.

In the Bible, Stephen was a man of God serving the community. When his co-workers in the gospel became jealous, they lied on him and caused him to be stoned by the Jewish community. He lost his life, but he never lost the love or unity of Christ and fulfilled his purpose in the earth. Weapons formed against him did not prosper, as he was immediately in the hands of the Lord and his journey came to an end that was pleasing to God and influential for the kingdom.

When Christ died on the cross, he saved us all from sin. There is no one that will be treated any differently. Grace and salvation are available to all. In the same spirit, our sacrificial love should be a beacon that draws others to us. Our kindness should be evident, and our good works should go before us. Our communications should be pleasant and filled with grace.

The way we show up, serve and make decisions should not be determined by the audience but more so by the provider of all life, the creator of all we know, and the keeper of our souls. All that God teaches us, comes down to one key behavior, love others as we love God and ourselves.

It can be hard to see ourselves in those we have markable differences with, especially those who try to hurt us on a regular basis. But it is when we can show the love of God to those who intentionally try to harm us, that God is able to do his greatest work. It is only then, when those who do not know God are able to witness his influence in our lives.

God desires that we choose peace and love above all else. When we take the high road of peace, and the pleasant road of love, God ensures that no weapon formed against us is able to prosper. He encamps his angels around us in protection. He protects us from dangers seen and unseen. Why? Because we are his children, his ambassadors, performing his will on earth. We are seated in heavenly places because we understand the depth and breadth of our actions. When we are handling God's business, bringing glory to his name, men glorify our actions and give God praise because our light has shone brightly before them, bringing blessing and honor with it. This can only be accomplished when we walk in peace, and choose a path of love. When we become perfect conduits of God's message and love, we are doing his will above our own. We know those we communicate and interact with may not believe as we do, but that is not our concern. Our concern is to become all that God created us to be and do so with one audience in mind, our Heavenly Father.

Let us then also let our communications align with the desired actions of God. Let us speak life, and good will. Let us speak the holy scriptures that we may spiritually prepared, doing so frequently throughout the day, arming us for the war that may occur within our own bodies. For we are natural men, unprepared for spiritual war. We must then arm ourselves each day, by putting on the full armor of God that we may be ready and available for the use of God when the time comes. We must steal away to our secret place, pray, and study the word of God at every opportunity. Rest in the power of the Holy Spirit, asking him for guidance and direction. Praise God before men, let them know we are children of the Most High God.

But let us not be fooled. God is a good God, filled with

amazement and wonder. His way leads to a life of adventure, satisfaction, and beautiful days filled with the desires of our hearts. But his way will also lead us onto terrains and areas that are filled with darkness that we may shine a light in dark places. In those days, we will suffer the scrutiny and disrespect of those who desire to dismiss, dismantle, and disregard the spirit of God on the earth.

We are his workmanship, prepared to do his will in the earth. No weapon formed against us shall prosper, every tongue that rises against us he will condemn. Know this, we are prepared for such a time as this. We did not choose God, he chose us, prepared us, and sent us. Therefore, we must choose to enjoy life, embrace peace, give love, and walk in the light, knowing that we are ambassadors of Christ and this is the true gift of life. God is intentional and we have been prepared for such a time as this.

To receive the gift of salvation that leads to eternal life, we must only confess and believe in our hearts that Christ died for us. But to gain access to an abundant life, filled with wisdom, stature and honor, we must place God first and be about His business.

Most Gracious and Heavenly Father,

How precious are Your thoughts toward us, O God! How vast is the sum of them! (1) Every good gift and every perfect gift is from above, coming down from the Father of lights with whom there is no variation or shadow due to change. (2) Therefore, we are thankful in all circumstances, for this is God's will for us who belong to Christ Jesus. (3) Just as we received Christ Jesus as Lord, we continue to live in him, strengthened in the faith as we were taught, and overflowing with thankfulness. (4) We trust in the LORD with all our hearts, and do not lean on our own understanding. In all our ways we acknowledge him, and he will make straight our paths. (5) We will not be conformed to this world, but be transformed by the renewal of our minds, that by testing we may discern what is the will of God, what is good and acceptable and perfect. (6) And it is our prayer that our love may abound more and more, with knowledge and all discernment, so that we may approve what is excellent, and so be pure and blameless for the day of Christ. (7)

The Spirit of the Lord will rest on us—the Spirit of wisdom and of understanding, the Spirit of counsel and of might, the Spirit of the knowledge and fear of the Lord—and we will delight in the fear of the Lord. (8)

For just as the body is one and has many members, and all the members of the body, though many, are one body, so it is with Christ. For the body does not consist of one member but of many. (10) When the Spirit of truth, comes, he will guide us into all the truth. He will not speak on his own; he will speak only what he hears, and he will tell us what is yet to come. (11) Blessed are they that trust in the Lord, and whose hope the Lord is. (12) Rather, we must grow in the grace and knowledge of our Lord and Savior Jesus Christ. All glory to him, both now and forever! (13) Oh, that you would bless us and enlarge our territory! Let your hand be with us, and keep us from harm so that we will be free from pain. (14)

In Jesus Name,
Amen

3

BLIND ANGER

When Delilah saw that he had told her everything, she sent word to the rulers of the Philistines, "Come back once more; he has told me everything." So the rulers of the Philistines returned with the silver in their hands. After putting him to sleep on her lap, she called for someone to shave off the seven braids of his hair, and so began to subdue him. And his strength left him.

Judges 16:18-19

Anger can blind us. When we do not learn to let go of what temporarily hurts us, we open the gate for more pain to seep through. If we aren't careful, it will completely consume us. Samson was prone to anger and often allowed anger to fuel his vengeance.

Ignoring a problem will not make it go away.

Samson loved women. He also loved his strength. His strength was given by God and there was a secret to his strength. For a long time, Samson fell privy to the desires of the women in his life and at times would find himself revealing things to them that should never be shared.

Samson knew that Delilah was up to no good. He also knew that she was relentless in her pursuit of his secrets. So, he gave in and told her what she wanted to know. As a result he was captured by his enemy. Unfortunately, his enemy was also the enemy of God's people and his irresponsible actions resulted in a punishment that not only hurt him but also the people he loved.

While in prison, Samson's captors cursed and taunted him. They made him the butt of their jokes. They beat him and caused him to become blind. They kept him in chains.

But as his captivity continued, Samson became strong. His hair grew, which was the secret to his strength. Even though this secret had been revealed to his enemy, they forgot and did not keep his hair cut while in captivity.

One day, they brought Samson from his cell to serve as entertainment for a festival. More than 3,000 Philistines were present. As they laughed and taunted him, Samson, whose strength had returned decided to kill them that day. He pushed the pillars of the pavilion in which he stood center, causing the great building to fall and kill all of those in proximity, including Samson himself.

Samson failed to keep God first in his life. He allowed his love for women to take precedence. Instead of living an abundant life of peace and tranquility, he ended his days in blind anger. He not only destroyed the life of his enemy, but he also took his own life in the process.

To receive the gift of salvation that leads to eternal life, we must only confess and believe in our hearts that Christ died for us. But to gain access to an abundant life, filled with wisdom, stature and honor, we must place God first and be about His business.

Most Gracious and Heavenly Father,

How precious are Your thoughts toward us, O God! How vast is the sum of them! (1) Every good gift and every perfect gift is from above, coming down from the Father of lights with whom there is no variation or shadow due to change. (2) Therefore, we are thankful in all circumstances, for this is God's will for us who belong to Christ Jesus. (3) Just as we received Christ Jesus as Lord, we continue to live in him, strengthened in the faith as we were taught, and overflowing with thankfulness. (4) We trust in the LORD with all our hearts, and do not lean on our own understanding. In all our ways we acknowledge him, and he will make straight our paths. (5) We will not be conformed to this world, but be transformed by the renewal of our minds, that by testing we may discern what is the will of God, what is good and acceptable and perfect. (6) And it is our prayer that our love may abound more and more, with knowledge and all discernment, so that we may approve what is excellent, and so be pure and blameless for the day of Christ. (7)

The Spirit of the Lord will rest on us—the Spirit of wisdom and of understanding, the Spirit of counsel and of might, the Spirit of the knowledge and fear of the Lord—and we will delight in the fear of the Lord. (8)

We cast down all bitterness, rage and anger, brawling and slander, along with every form of malice. (15) Instead let us be quick to listen, slow to speak and slow to become angry, because human anger does not produce the righteousness that God desires. (16) For fools give full vent to their rage, but the wise bring calm in the end. (17) A person's wisdom yields patience; it is to one's glory to overlook an offense. (18) So let us refrain from anger, turn from wrath, and do not fret—it leads only to evil. For those who are evil will be destroyed, but those who hope in the LORD will inherit the land. (19) Our shield is God Most High, who saves the upright in heart. God is a righteous judge, a God who displays his wrath every day. (20) Whoever is pregnant with evil conceives trouble and gives birth to disillusionment. Whoever digs a hole and scoops it out falls into the pit they have made. The trouble they cause recoils on them; their violence comes down on their own heads. We will give thanks to the Lord because of his righteousness. We will sing the praises of the name of the Lord Most High.

In Jesus Name,
Amen

4

PRIORITIES

After Jesus said this, he looked toward heaven and prayed:

"Father, the hour has come. Glorify your Son, that your Son may glorify you. For you granted him authority over all people that he might give eternal life to all those you have given him. Now this is eternal life: that they know you, the only true God, and Jesus Christ, whom you have sent. I have brought you glory on earth by finishing the work you gave me to do. And now, Father, glorify me in your presence with the glory I had with you before the world began."

"Righteous Father, though the world does not know you, I know you, and they know that you have sent me. I have made you known to them, and will continue to make you known in order that the love you have for me may be in them and that I myself may be in them."

John 1:1-5, 25-26

It is critical that we understand what gives and brings life to us and others. A relationship with Jesus Christ, the Holy Spirit and our Heavenly Father brings a confident hope to all.

Jesus lived a short meaningful life on earth. He understood that he could not complete his assignment on earth without being connected to God. A connection to God does not mean that we will not endure hardship, it simply means that when we endure hardship, we will know how to respond.

God is our source. He is the only one that is able to accurately direct us at all times. He knows and understands every circumstance we may face. Our confidence not only lies in his omniscience, but also in his omnibenevolence. God knows, he cares and he lives.

Therefore, we must prioritize our relationship with God. Just as Jesus spent quality time with God in his secret places, we too must spend quality time with God. This means we praise God when we can, we pray to God when we can, and we commune with the Holy Spirit.

Praise is a sweet smelling sacrifice to God. It comes from our hearts and lingers in the atmosphere. It echoes in our minds, long after we have sang the verses and the melodies strum within our hearts throughout the day.

Prayer strengthens us. It reminds us of every promise God has made to us in the Bible. It is life giving and confidence building. We stand firmly on the Word of God knowing it cannot fail us. Our faith is what exponentially binds the word of God to our works. It connects what we know, to what we hear, and cements what we believe, making a three fold cord that is not easily broken.

The Holy Spirit is within us. The Holy Spirit prays what we do not know to pray. We must release our own wisdom and allow the Holy Spirit to guide us at times. This requires intentionality. When we set time aside to welcome the Holy Spirit, and rest in his will, he begins to do amazing things through us that we could not imagine.

Just as Jesus prayed in John 17, we are to prioritize our relationship with God. It is the cornerstone and targeted center of our life. It is the one place from which all love flows. If we make God our center, everything else falls into place. Our confidence, joy, peace, rest, and love all begin with how we choose to intentionally love God and more importantly, accept his love for us.

To receive the gift of salvation that leads to eternal life, we must only confess and believe in our hearts that Christ

died for us. But to gain access to an abundant life, filled with wisdom, stature and honor, we must place God first and be about His business.

Most Gracious and Heavenly Father,

How precious are Your thoughts toward us, O God! How vast is the sum of them! (1) Every good gift and every perfect gift is from above, coming down from the Father of lights with whom there is no variation or shadow due to change. (2) Therefore, we are thankful in all circumstances, for this is God's will for us who belong to Christ Jesus. (3) Just as we received Christ Jesus as Lord, we continue to live in him, strengthened in the faith as we were taught, and overflowing with thankfulness. (4) We trust in the LORD with all our hearts, and do not lean on our own understanding. In all our ways we acknowledge him, and he will make straight our paths. (5) We will not be conformed to this world, but be transformed by the renewal of our minds, that by testing we may discern what is the will of God, what is good and acceptable and perfect. (6) And it is our prayer that our love may abound more and more, with knowledge and all discernment, so that we may approve what is excellent, and so be pure and blameless for the day of Christ. (7)

The Spirit of the Lord will rest on us—the Spirit of wisdom and of understanding, the Spirit of counsel and of might, the Spirit of the knowledge and fear of the Lord—and we will delight in the fear of the Lord. (8)

Whom have we in heaven but you? And there is nothing on earth that we desire besides you. Our flesh and our hearts may fail, but God is the strength of our heart and our portion forever. (22) For your grace is sufficient for us, your power is made perfect in our weakness. Therefore we will boast all the more gladly of our weaknesses, so that the power of Christ may rest upon us. (23) On God rests our salvation and our glory; our mighty rock, our refuge is God. (24) Therefore we who are joined to the Lord become one spirit with him. (25) We abide in you, and you in us. As the branch cannot bear fruit by itself, unless it abides in the vine, neither can we, unless we abide in you. You are the vine; we are the branches. Whoever abides in you and you in us, bear much fruit, for apart from you we can do nothing. (26)

In Jesus Name,
Amen

5

WISDOM

He who walks in integrity walks securely,
but he who perverts his ways will be found out.
Proverbs 10:9

We cannot survive day-to-day living in peace without wisdom and discernment. Wise people enjoy life. They create safe boundaries around themselves and prioritize what is important to God and what is important to them. They care and serve others from a selfless point of view. They do not steal or take what has not been earned, with idle yet greedy hands. They are blessed because they are willing to work diligently and do not brag about or bring shame to those who bless them.

Integrity reaps confidence. When we are doing what we are supposed to be doing, God is pleased and allows us to have honor with him and man. God intentionally shines a light on those who are walking as he commands.

Manipulation causes grief. People who feel like they are being used or taken advantage of become angry, distrustful and resentful toward those who manipulate them. They limit their communications, contact, and exposure to them.

Big mouths cause ruin. Everyone that is connected to you is not for you. Some are waiting and lying in secret to learn exactly what they need to know to destroy you. Discretion is a gift to those who are willing to rest beneath it's shadow. By accumulating knowledge, we prevent destruction.

Perversion is always found out. When we are operating

outside of the will of God, everyone around us watches our activities and decides whether we are truly ambassadors of Christ. It doesn't matter what we say, what matters is what we reflect through our actions. If we want to share the good news with others, we have to accept and love the good news ourselves. We can't live a life that dishonors God then claim the blessings of those who honor God. God will not be mocked. To whom much is given, much is required.

Wisdom and discernment are gifts that God gives to those who love and keep him first, those who honor him with wholeness and truth. God is our teacher, he helps us to know exactly what to do and when to do it.

To receive the gift of salvation that leads to eternal life, we must only confess and believe in our hearts that Christ died for us. But to gain access to an abundant life, filled with wisdom, stature and honor, we must place God first and be about His business.

Most Gracious and Heavenly Father,

How precious are Your thoughts toward us, O God! How vast is the sum of them! (1) Every good gift and every perfect gift is from above, coming down from the Father of lights with whom there is no variation or shadow due to change. (2) Therefore, we are thankful in all circumstances, for this is God's will for us who belong to Christ Jesus. (3) Just as we received Christ Jesus as Lord, we continue to live in him, strengthened in the faith as we were taught, and overflowing with thankfulness. (4) We trust in the LORD with all our hearts, and do not lean on our own understanding. In all our ways we acknowledge him, and he will make straight our paths. (5) We will not be conformed to this world, but be transformed by the renewal of our minds, that by testing we may discern what is the will of God, what is good and acceptable and perfect. (6) And it is our prayer that our love may abound more and more, with knowledge and all discernment, so that we may approve what is excellent, and so be pure and blameless for the day of Christ. (7)

The Spirit of the Lord will rest on us—the Spirit of wisdom and of understanding, the Spirit of counsel and of might, the Spirit of the knowledge and fear of the Lord—and we will delight in the fear of the Lord. (8)

The natural person does not accept the things of the Spirit of God, for they are folly to him, and he is not able to understand them because they are spiritually discerned. (27) But the wisdom from above is first pure, then peaceable, gentle, open to reason, full of mercy and good fruits, impartial and sincere. (28) Therefore we pray that our love may abound more and more, with knowledge and all discernment, so that we may approve what is excellent, and so be pure and blameless for the day of Christ. (29) We pray for the Lord to give us an understanding mind to govern his people, that we may discern between good and evil, for who is able to govern your great people? (30) Lord, you are sending us you out as sheep in the midst of wolves, so teach us to be wise as serpents and innocent as doves. (31)

In Jesus Name,
Amen

6

REFLECTIONS OF LIGHT

Therefore be imitators of God, as beloved children; and walk in love, just as Christ also loved you and gave Himself up for us, an offering and a sacrifice to God as a fragrant aroma.
Ephesians 5:1-2

There are three ways to reflect light. Diffuse reflection scatters light at many angles and generally allows for more color to be distributed because most of the objects the light hits are solid colors and therefore reflect light diffusely. Specular reflection reflects light at the same angle by which the light strikes the surface, giving what it lands upon a mirror or glossy effect. A glossy reflection falls into porous objects that contain divets or pockets and therefore reflect light specularly and diffusely, making what it falls upon appear glossy. (37)

Specular Reflection of Light

When we simply choose to honor God and become as much like him as possible, we shine our lights specularly. As those who love God, and worship Him, and have become His friends, God reveals knowledge, insight, and spiritual wonder to us. He shares an intimacy with each of us in ways that are unique, individual, and meaningful. Much like a man and woman connect when married, as members of the body of Christ, we share like-mindedness with God when we are connected to him

Diffuse Reflection of Light

So when we find ourselves exposed to the sinful culture that exists in the world: perversion, addiction, obsessions, power, violence, and greed - we should be as disgusted and offended by it as God is. We should dislike and distance ourselves from overt sin and sinful behavior.

As we grow to understand the will of God, in our private worship, we become more like him in public places. What used to entertain us is no longer entertaining. What used to be a bad habit for us has become a place of dishonor, shame, and disgust. We instead choose to be filled with humility and grace that Jesus Christ exemplified. We choose to have love and respect for others, and consideration and compassion for those who are without. We choose to shine a light on evil because in doing so, we bring value to the light.

Glossy Reflection of Light
Our public worship of Christ, through our walk (not our talk), reflects God in specular ways. When we choose to do so, while also extending the grace, mercy, and kindness of God to those who treat the people of God and the act of being holy with gross disdain, disrespect, and disgust, we are pouring light into the cracks, crevices, and divots of life. When we pray for those who despitefully use us, take advantage of our kindness, and love them with consistency, we are reflecting His light in glossy ways.

Regardless of how we choose to reflect the light of God, our commitment is required. God loves us. He is committed to us. He will never change. As his ambassadors, as those committed to sharing the gospel, we are to be consistent as well. We are to choose who we are going to serve, God or man. If we choose God, as he has chosen us, we are committed to him as a husband that has committed to a wife. We have become one, and to disrespect God, is to disrespect ourselves.

To receive the gift of salvation that leads to eternal life, we must only confess and believe in our hearts that Christ died for us. But to gain access to an abundant life, filled with wisdom, stature and honor, we must place God first and be about His business.

Most Gracious and Heavenly Father,

How precious are Your thoughts toward us, O God! How vast is the sum of them! (1) Every good gift and every perfect gift is from above, coming down from the Father of lights with whom there is no variation or shadow due to change. (2) Therefore, we are thankful in all circumstances, for this is God's will for us who belong to Christ Jesus. (3) Just as we received Christ Jesus as Lord, we continue to live in him, strengthened in the faith as we were taught, and overflowing with thankfulness. (4) We trust in the LORD with all our hearts, and do not lean on our own understanding. In all our ways we acknowledge him, and he will make straight our paths. (5) We will not be conformed to this world, but be transformed by the renewal of our minds, that by testing we may discern what is the will of God, what is good and acceptable and perfect. (6) And it is our prayer that our love may abound more and more, with knowledge and all discernment, so that we may approve what is excellent, and so be pure and blameless for the day of Christ. (7)

The Spirit of the Lord will rest on us—the Spirit of wisdom and of understanding, the Spirit of counsel and of might, the Spirit of the knowledge and fear of the Lord—and we will delight in the fear of the Lord. (8)

Therefore, as we received Christ Jesus the Lord, so we walk in him. (38) In order that the righteous requirement of the law might be fulfilled in us, we walk not according to the flesh but according to the Spirit. (39) By this is love perfected with us, so that we may have confidence for the day of judgment, because as he is so also are we in this world. (40) For if we live, we live to the Lord, and if we die, we die to the Lord. So then, whether we live or whether we die, we are the Lord's. (41) Now may the God of peace himself sanctify us completely, and may our whole spirit and soul and body be kept blameless at the coming of our Lord Jesus Christ. (42)

In Jesus Name,
Amen

7

SPIRITUALLY ALERT

However, when the people of Gibeon heard what Joshua had done to Jericho and Ai, they resorted to a ruse: They went as a delegation whose donkeys were loaded with worn-out sacks and old wineskins, cracked and mended. They put worn and patched sandals on their feet and wore old clothes. All the bread of their food supply was dry and moldy. Then they went to Joshua in the camp at Gilgal and said to him and the Israelites, "We have come from a distant country; make a treaty with us."

—

The Israelites sampled their provisions but did not inquire of the Lord. Then Joshua made a treaty of peace with them to let them live, and the leaders of the assembly ratified it by oath.

Joshua 9:3-6, 14-15

It is every Christian's hope to be in right-standing with God. We want to live a life that pleases Him and embodies the characteristics Christ exemplified in the earth. However, even when we are diligent in seeking Him, spending time with Him and calling on Him, we can still miss the mark.

Joshua and the Israelites, had just won battles against Jericho and Ai. They'd recently renewed their covenant with God with a respectful and symbolic ceremony as instructed through the Word of God. They were confident that they were in right standing with God.

But they were fooled by a local enemy who decided to take the road less traveled by tricking the Israelites rather than facing them in battle. The Israelites were caught off guard and rather than seek the Lord for guidance, they attempted to manage the situation based on their own knowledge.

As Christians, we face unique situations, conversations, and opportunities day in and day out. But we must be careful not to mistake our ritualistic times that we worship God as the sole preparation for any and every battle. Our consistent worship may be a morning prayer, a morning devotional or simply listening to gospel music and giving God praise each afternoon.

No matter what we do, we must not mistake those activities with seeking the wisdom, discernment, and guidance of God to make important decisions each day.

Yes, God is with us. Yes, God cares for us. Yes, God is always for us. But God wants to make sure we are always seeking him for guidance. He sees the work of our enemies. He knows what they are planning and how they operate. Only in this way, can we remain spiritually alert and ready for any situation that comes our way.

We all have a unique purpose and way to accomplish God's will in the earth. But not one of us can do so with confidence, assurance, and success without first seeking God in all matters. We cannot allow our decisions to be misled by emotion, logic, or physical sense (natural defenses) but only by the spiritual discernment the Holy Spirit provides.

To receive the gift of salvation that leads to eternal life, we must only confess and believe in our hearts that Christ died for us. But to gain access to an abundant life, filled with wisdom, stature and honor, we must place God first and be about His business.

Most Gracious and Heavenly Father,

How precious are Your thoughts toward us, O God! How vast is the sum of them! (1) Every good gift and every perfect gift is from above, coming down from the Father of lights with whom there is no variation or shadow due to change. (2) Therefore, we are thankful in all circumstances, for this is God's will for us who belong to Christ Jesus. (3) Just as we received Christ Jesus as Lord, we continue to live in him, strengthened in the faith as we were taught, and overflowing with thankfulness. (4) We trust in the LORD with all our hearts, and do not lean on our own understanding. In all our ways we acknowledge him, and he will make straight our paths. (5) We will not be conformed to this world, but be transformed by the renewal of our minds, that by testing we may discern what is the will of God, what is good and acceptable and perfect. (6) And it is our prayer that our love may abound more and more, with knowledge and all discernment, so that we may approve what is excellent, and so be pure and blameless for the day of Christ. (7)

The Spirit of the Lord will rest on us—the Spirit of wisdom and of understanding, the Spirit of counsel and of might, the Spirit of the knowledge and fear of the Lord—and we will delight in the fear of the Lord. (8)

Let no one deceive us with empty words, for because of such things God's wrath comes on those who are disobedient. We will not be partners with them. (43) As your beloved, we do not believe every spirit, but test the spirits to see whether they are from God, for many false prophets have gone out into the world. (44) We do not give dogs what is sacred; we do not throw our pearls to pigs. If we do, they may trample them under their feet, and turn and tear us to pieces. (45) Oh, the depth of the riches of the wisdom and knowledge of God! How unsearchable his judgments, and his paths beyond tracing out! "Who has known the mind of the Lord? Or who has been his counselor? Who has ever given to God, that God should repay them? For from him and through him and for him are all things. To him be the glory forever! (46)

In Jesus Name,
Amen

8

WITHOUT A DOUBT

Shadrach, Meshach and Abednego replied to him,
"King Nebuchadnezzar, we do not need to defend ourselves before
you in this matter. If we are thrown into the blazing furnace, the God
we serve is able to deliver us from it, and he will deliver us from Your
Majesty's hand. But even if he does not, we want you to know, Your
Majesty, that we will not serve your gods or worship the image of gold
you have set up."
Daniel 3:16-18

What is it that you want others to know about your God? Shadrach, Meshach and Abednego wanted the king to know that regardless of their outcome, they would not bow down to the king's gods or the image of gold he'd erected.

Shadrach, Meshach, and Abednego had just been promoted to positions of power and authority. Many thought because they'd been given this opportunity that there would be no doubt they would acquiesce to whatever the king commanded. When the king built a golden image of himself and issued a decree throughout the province of Babylon, he expected everyone to adhere to it. But the king and his other magistrates did not realize, recognize or remember that Shadrach, Meshach and Abednego were summoned with Daniel before he'd interpreted the dream of the king.

When Daniel spoke to the king, he told him what God revealed.

"Your Majesty, you are the king of kings. The God of heaven has given
you dominion and power and might and glory; in your hands he has
placed all mankind and the beasts of the field and the birds in the sky.

Wherever they live, he has made you ruler over them all. You are that head of gold."

Daniel 2:36-38

It was God who'd given King Nebuchadnezzar dominion and named him the king of kings, and had recently revealed the future of the kingdom to the king (depicted with a statue of his kingdom that was not solid in gold, but with mixed minerals which indicated the breaking off the kingdom into separate divisions and falling under new leadership). Shadrach, Meshach and Abednego recognized that the king was making a big mistake challenging the authority, sovereignty, and ability of the God they served. They being assigned to positions of leadership were willing to sacrifice their lives in order to reflect and show what great leadership does. Leaders stand behind what is right when it is right - even at the risk of his or her own life.

To receive the gift of salvation that leads to eternal life, we must only confess and believe in our hearts that Christ died for us. But to gain access to an abundant life, filled with wisdom, stature, and honor, we must place God first and be about His business.

Most Gracious and Heavenly Father,

How precious are Your thoughts toward us, O God! How vast is the sum of them! (1) Every good gift and every perfect gift is from above, coming down from the Father of lights with whom there is no variation or shadow due to change. (2) Therefore, we are thankful in all circumstances, for this is God's will for us who belong to Christ Jesus. (3) Just as we received Christ Jesus as Lord, we continue to live in him, strengthened in the faith as we were taught, and overflowing with thankfulness. (4) We trust in the LORD with all our hearts, and do not lean on our own understanding. In all our ways we acknowledge him, and he will make straight our paths. (5) We will not be conformed to this world, but be transformed by the renewal of our minds, that by testing we may discern what is the will of God, what is good and acceptable and perfect. (6) And it is our prayer that our love may abound more and more, with knowledge and all discernment, so that we may approve what is excellent, and so be pure and blameless for the day of Christ. (7)

The Spirit of the Lord will rest on us—the Spirit of wisdom and of understanding, the Spirit of counsel and of might, the Spirit of the knowledge and fear of the Lord—and we will delight in the fear of the Lord. (8)

And this is the confidence that we have toward him, that if we ask anything according to his will he hears us. (47) Now faith is the assurance of things hoped for, the conviction of things not seen. (48) Therefore, we confess our sins to one another and pray for one another, that we may be healed. The prayer of a righteous person has great power as it is working. (49) Supplications, prayers, intercessions, and thanksgivings will be made for all people, for kings and all who are in high positions, that we may lead a peaceful and quiet life, godly and dignified in every way. (50) For without faith it is impossible to please God, for whoever would draw near to God must believe that he exists and that he rewards those who seek him. (51)

In Jesus Name,
Amen

9

END WELL

For I will not trust in my bow, neither shall my sword save me.

Psalm 44:6

King Asa spent most of his reign as the king of Judah honoring God. He kept God first and God blessed him in battle and gave his land peace. But after many years, Baasha, the king of Israel came against him. King Baasha began to build a strong wall outside of Ramah, to keep anyone from coming in or going out of Judah.

In response, King Asa called upon a neighboring king to help him. He sent gold from the church's treasury to King Ben-Hadad of Aram, who had a strong army. King Ben-Hadad agreed to help King Asa. Aram then successfully attacked the Israelite armies and stopped all work on the wall in Ramah. King Asa used the resources left by King Baasha to build up his other cities in Judah.

But God was not pleased. He sent a seer to give King Asa a message.

"Because you relied on the king of Aram and not on the Lord your God, the army of the king of Aram has escaped from your hand. Were not the Cushites and Libyans a mighty army with great numbers of chariots and horsemen? Yet when you relied on the Lord, he delivered them into your hand. For the eyes of the Lord range throughout the earth to strengthen those whose hearts are fully committed to him. You have done a foolish thing, and from now on you will be at war."

2 Chronicles 16:7-9

King Asa was so angry at the prophet that he threw him in prison. He was so angry that his anger seeped onto those he was purposed to protect and honor. Soon after, King Asa was bowed down with severe disease and eventually died. Despite his unending pain, he never repented or called on God again. Instead, he remained angry at God until his dying day.

There was a time when King Asa saw great value in his relationship with God. He trusted God without question and his boasting was in God. But eventually, (after years of God-given peace) he felt as though he understood how to resolve his own problems and did not need the assistance of God. Once called out on it, instead of repenting for his sins, he resolved that being his form of right, albeit temporarily, was more important than humbling himself and acquiescing to what he knew was right.

We all have a choice, we can choose to honor God with our lives, submitting to His will or we can be wise in our own eyes, living a life that is filled with pain, regret, and misunderstanding. God is faithful to forgive us if we repent. His grace is sufficient. We can lean on Him, he will not let us down.

To receive the gift of salvation that leads to eternal life, we must only confess and believe in our hearts that Christ died for us. But to gain access to an abundant life, filled with wisdom, stature, and honor, we must place God first and be about His business.

Most Gracious and Heavenly Father,

How precious are Your thoughts toward us, O God! How vast is the sum of them! (1) Every good gift and every perfect gift is from above, coming down from the Father of lights with whom there is no variation or shadow due to change. (2) Therefore, we are thankful in all circumstances, for this is God's will for us who belong to Christ Jesus. (3) Just as we received Christ Jesus as Lord, we continue to live in him, strengthened in the faith as we were taught, and overflowing with thankfulness. (4) We trust in the LORD with all our hearts, and do not lean on our own understanding. In all our ways we acknowledge him, and he will make straight our paths. (5) We will not be conformed to this world, but be transformed by the renewal of our minds, that by testing we may discern what is the will of God, what is good and acceptable and perfect. (6) And it is our prayer that our love may abound more and more, with knowledge and all discernment, so that we may approve what is excellent, and so be pure and blameless for the day of Christ. (7)

The Spirit of the Lord will rest on us—the Spirit of wisdom and of understanding, the Spirit of counsel and of might, the Spirit of the knowledge and fear of the Lord—and we will delight in the fear of the Lord. (8)

You are our King and our God, who decrees victories for Jacob. Through you we push back our enemies; through your name we trample our foes. We put no trust in our bows, our sword does not bring us victory; but you give us victory over our enemies, you put our adversaries to shame. In God we make our boast all day long, and we will praise your name forever. (52)

In Jesus Name,
Amen

10

INTENTIONAL WORSHIP AND WISDOM

See, I have chosen Bezalel son of Uri, the son of Hur,
of the tribe of Judah, and I have filled him with the Spirit of God, with
wisdom, with understanding, with knowledge and with all kinds of
skills— to make artistic designs for work in gold, silver and bronze, to
cut and set stones, to work in wood, and to engage in all kinds of crafts.
Moreover, I have appointed Oholiab son of Ahisamak,
of the tribe of Dan, to help him.

Exodus 31:2-6

Bezalel and Oholiab were anointed and gifted by the Holy Spirit to create the foundational worship artifacts that would visually indicate the presence of God was near. The list of artifacts they were responsible for creating are below.

- The Tent of Meeting
- The Ark of the Covenant Law with the Atonement Cover
- The Furnishings for the Tent of Meeting: Table and its articles; Pure Gold Lamp Stand and accessories; Altar of Incense; Altar of Burnt Offering and utensils; Basin with its stand
- Priestly Woven Garments: Sacred garments and garments for the sons of Aaron
- The Anointing Oil
- Fragrant Incense for the Holy Place

God chose those who were willing to be filled with the Holy Spirit that they may receive His wisdom and gifts that would prepare them to do his will so that the people of God could worship Him with a form of understanding.

Every good gift and every perfect gift is from above, and comes down from the Father of lights, with whom there is no variation or shadow of turning.
James 1:17

After the artifacts were made, God taught Moses the importance of honoring the Sabbath. He shared,

Then the Lord said to Moses, "Say to the Israelites, 'You must observe my Sabbaths. This will be a sign between me and you for the generations to come, so you may know that I am the Lord, who makes you holy."
Exodus 31:12-13

After sharing the importance of the Sabbath, God inscribed the Ten Commandments and gave them to Moses.

Wisdom is a gift that God gives to those who wish to receive it. But to receive wisdom that is holy, it must be given by God through worship and used to bring about His purpose. Our wisdom is not for a paycheck, or our survival, God provides all that we need. Our wisdom is used to build the kingdom of God on earth and to shine a light on his presence in our lives. Our wisdom is used to bring him glory and only through giving God the glory is wisdom received.

The Sabbath is an intentional day of worship. It is a day of restoration and reflection. It allows us to consider what God has done and what he will do, or desires for us to do. It is a day to bring glory to God through our actions. It is a day when we can place God first, giving him a tithe of our time as he has instructed through the commandments. To honor the Sabbath is to obey God.

To receive the gift of salvation that leads to eternal life, we must only confess and believe in our hearts that Christ died for us. But to gain access to an abundant life, filled with wisdom, stature, and honor, we must place God first and be about His business.

Most Gracious and Heavenly Father,

How precious are Your thoughts toward us, O God! How vast is the sum of them! (1) Every good gift and every perfect gift is from above, coming down from the Father of lights with whom there is no variation or shadow due to change. (2) Therefore, we are thankful in all circumstances, for this is God's will for us who belong to Christ Jesus. (3) Just as we received Christ Jesus as Lord, we continue to live in him, strengthened in the faith as we were taught, and overflowing with thankfulness. (4) We trust in the LORD with all our hearts, and do not lean on our own understanding. In all our ways we acknowledge him, and he will make straight our paths. (5) We will not be conformed to this world, but be transformed by the renewal of our minds, that by testing we may discern what is the will of God, what is good and acceptable and perfect. (6) And it is our prayer that our love may abound more and more, with knowledge and all discernment, so that we may approve what is excellent, and so be pure and blameless for the day of Christ. (7)

The Spirit of the Lord will rest on us—the Spirit of wisdom and of understanding, the Spirit of counsel and of might, the Spirit of the knowledge and fear of the Lord—and we will delight in the fear of the Lord. (8)

Our Father in heaven, hallowed be your name, your kingdom come, your will be done, on earth as it is in heaven. Give us today our daily bread. And forgive us our debts, as we also have forgiven our debtors. And lead us not into temptation, but deliver us from the evil one. (53)

In Jesus Name,
Amen

11
GENERATIONAL LEADERSHIP

Go and inquire of the Lord for me and for the remnant in Israel and Judah about what is written in this book that has been found. Great is the Lord's anger that is poured out on us because those who have gone before us have not kept the word of the Lord; they have not acted in accordance with all that is written in this book.

2 Chronicles 34:21

Josiah was the youngest king in Jerusalem, named king at only eight years old. Yet, he was also one of the wisest. By the time he was 16, he'd committed himself to seeking the wisdom of God and was determined to ensure the kingdom honored God. He removed all of the areas of idol worship and destroyed any visible remnants of idols. By age 24, he was determined to restore the temple of God and provided resources and instructions to do so. As the offerings were gathered for restoration of the temple, the workers found the book of the Law that had been given to Moses. At the reading of the law, King Josiah was stressed and concerned as he realized his people were still choosing to worship other gods and were sinning before the Lord. He immediately inquired of the Lord for guidance on how to respond.

When the prophet sent word back to King Josiah, it was revealed that destruction had been determined and Jerusalem would definitely fall. Josiah had the book read before all of his people and called for repentance. But because of Josiah's humble nature and responsive heart, he would not be a witness to the fall nor would he experience it.

After King Josiah passed away, his son, Jehoiakim became king and ruled for four years, he too was sent a message from the prophet, Jeremiah. Jeremiah's message was read by his scribe,

Baruch, in the church on the day of fasting. When the priests heard the message, they had it read before the people. When the son of the king's secretary heard it, he went and told his father. His father and his friends eventually called for Baruch the messenger who'd read the message in the church. They asked him to read the message to them aloud.

After hearing the message, the men in great fear took it to the king. The king burned the scroll as sections were read to him, he was unconcerned and unbothered. This angered God. He'd sent this message as an opportunity for repentance. Instead, the king ignored him. He sent Jeremiah another message to be delivered to the man who burned the scroll.

"Take another scroll and write on it all the words that were on the first scroll, which Jehoiakim king of Judah burned up. Also tell Jehoiakim king of Judah, 'This is what the Lord says: You burned that scroll and said, "Why did you write on it that the king of Babylon would certainly come and destroy this land and wipe from it both man and beast?" Therefore this is what the Lord says about Jehoiakim king of Judah: He will have no one to sit on the throne of David; his body will be thrown out and exposed to the heat by day and the frost by night. I will punish him and his children and his attendants for their wickedness; I will bring on them and those living in Jerusalem and the people of Judah every disaster I pronounced against them, because they have not listened.'"

Jeremiah 36:28-31

God is faithful to grant us an opportunity to repent for our sins. He gives us a way to turn ship and change direction. But those who are defiant believe that whatever they want to do is perfectly fine because they cannot see God's hand at work. Rather than give honor to God and repent, they stand in defiance with a heart of stone and a stiff neck, rendering pain and hurt not just for themselves but also their descendants that follow. God gives us opportunities to render generational blessings or generational curses. We choose the destinies of those that follow us by our response to God.

To receive the gift of salvation that leads to eternal life, we must only confess and believe in our hearts that Christ

died for us. But to gain access to an abundant life, filled with wisdom, stature, and honor, we must place God first and be about His business.

Most Gracious and Heavenly Father,

How precious are Your thoughts toward us, O God! How vast is the sum of them! (1) Every good gift and every perfect gift is from above, coming down from the Father of lights with whom there is no variation or shadow due to change. (2) Therefore, we are thankful in all circumstances, for this is God's will for us who belong to Christ Jesus. (3) Just as we received Christ Jesus as Lord, we continue to live in him, strengthened in the faith as we were taught, and overflowing with thankfulness. (4) We trust in the LORD with all our hearts, and do not lean on our own understanding. In all our ways we acknowledge him, and he will make straight our paths. (5) We will not be conformed to this world, but be transformed by the renewal of our minds, that by testing we may discern what is the will of God, what is good and acceptable and perfect. (6) And it is our prayer that our love may abound more and more, with knowledge and all discernment, so that we may approve what is excellent, and so be pure and blameless for the day of Christ. (7)

The Spirit of the Lord will rest on us—the Spirit of wisdom and of understanding, the Spirit of counsel and of might, the Spirit of the knowledge and fear of the Lord—and we will delight in the fear of the Lord. (8)

We are your people, your inheritance that you brought out by your great power and your outstretched arm. (54) We seek your favor Lord, please hear our prayer, see our oppressors and provide deliverance that we may escape. (55) For evildoers are overwhelmed with dread, for God is present in the company of the righteous. (56) We praise you Lord. Blessed are we who fear the Lord, who find great delight in you commands. Our children will be mighty in the land; the generation of the upright will be blessed. Wealth and riches are in our houses, and our righteousness endures forever. Even in darkness light dawns for the upright, for those who are gracious and compassionate and righteous. Good will come to those who are generous and lend freely, who conduct their affairs with justice. Surely the righteous will never be shaken; we will be remembered forever. We will have no fear of bad news; our hearts are steadfast, trusting in the Lord. Our hearts are secure, we will have no fear; in the end we will look in triumph on our foes. We have freely scattered our gifts to the poor, our righteousness endures forever; our horn will be lifted high in honor. The wicked will see and be vexed, they will gnash their teeth and waste away; the longings of the wicked will come to nothing. (57)

In Jesus Name,
Amen

12

GIVING AND INHERITANCE

*Jesus looked at him and loved him. "One thing you lack," he said.
"Go, sell everything you have and give to the poor, and you will have
treasure in heaven. Then come, follow me."*

Mark 10:21

An inheritance is a gift someone receives after the giver
passes away. A gift is something someone receives while the giver
is still alive. The difference is the giver is able to see a gift being
used as it is received, while an inheritance is cherished after one
passes.

A young man asked Jesus, what he must do to inherit
eternal life. Jesus told him that he must sell all he has and give it
to the poor. Now this young man had lived a clean and righteous
life before God, following all of the commandments. He wanted
affirmation from Jesus that he was indeed righteous, but Jesus
challenged him to let go of what he wanted desperately to hold
on to. In this way, he could reflect true discipleship. But Jesus also
knew that this would be difficult for him and for anyone who
had great wealth to let go of what they had. Then he espoused a
promise.

*"Truly I tell you," Jesus replied, "no one who has left home or brothers
or sisters or mother or father or children or fields for me and the
gospel will fail to receive a hundred times as much in this present age:
homes, brothers, sisters, mothers, children and fields—along with
persecutions—and in the age to come eternal life. But many who are
first will be last, and the last first."*

Mark 10:29-31

The entire tenth chapter of Mark shares a reliable message, personal comfort is not the goal of a disciple - taking care of others is what is most important. In this way is God's love shared throughout the earth. Yet true sacrifice brings great pain and often, great anger.

In the beginning of the chapter, Jewish leaders asked Jesus about divorce. He told them that any man or woman that divorces and marries another has committed adultery and that divorce was an institution created by hard hearts. Then Jesus admonishes his disciples for sending children in need away. He tells them that the kingdom of God belongs to them. After a man calls him good, Jesus affirms that noone except God is good. Then he shares that only when we are willing to let go of all that we think is important (our happiness, peace, joy, and personal level of security) are we able to receive one hundred times more. But the abundant blessings do not arrive without great suffering. Then Jesus reminds his disciples that his end was near, but promised he would rise again. At this, two of his disciples demand (because they pulled Jesus to the side and told him give them what they asked for) that they sit on his right and left side in heaven. Jesus immediately shared that not only were they not capable of doing what was necessary to obtain such authority, they were not assigned to receive such glory as those spots were designated by a higher power. Finally, there was a blind man sitting by the road as Jesus and his disciples passed. His name was blind Bartimaeus. The people told him to be quiet, instead he shouted all the louder, "Jesus, son of David, have mercy on me!" That day, his faith made him whole.

For Jesus, to give took only a moment, but for blind Bartimaeus to receive, it was life-changing. We have the power to provide life-changing blessings to others, but it requires that we are willing to sacrifice our moments, our gifts, our increase, our comfort, and at times, our peace that others may see, feel, experience, and learn of the love of Christ.

To receive the gift of salvation that leads to eternal life, we must only confess and believe in our hearts that Christ

died for us. But to gain access to an abundant life, filled with wisdom, stature, and honor, we must place God first and be about His business.

Most Gracious and Heavenly Father,

How precious are Your thoughts toward us, O God! How vast is the sum of them! (1) Every good gift and every perfect gift is from above, coming down from the Father of lights with whom there is no variation or shadow due to change. (2) Therefore, we are thankful in all circumstances, for this is God's will for us who belong to Christ Jesus. (3) Just as we received Christ Jesus as Lord, we continue to live in him, strengthened in the faith as we were taught, and overflowing with thankfulness. (4) We trust in the LORD with all our hearts, and do not lean on our own understanding. In all our ways we acknowledge him, and he will make straight our paths. (5) We will not be conformed to this world, but be transformed by the renewal of our minds, that by testing we may discern what is the will of God, what is good and acceptable and perfect. (6) And it is our prayer that our love may abound more and more, with knowledge and all discernment, so that we may approve what is excellent, and so be pure and blameless for the day of Christ. (7)

The Spirit of the Lord will rest on us—the Spirit of wisdom and of understanding, the Spirit of counsel and of might, the Spirit of the knowledge and fear of the Lord—and we will delight in the fear of the Lord. (8)

We demolish arguments and every pretension that sets itself up against the knowledge of God, and we take captive every thought to make it obedient to Christ. (58) This calls for patient endurance on the part of the people of God who keep his commands and remain faithful to Jesus. (59) And this is love: that we walk in obedience to his commands. As we have heard from the beginning, his command is that we walk in love.(60)

In Jesus Name,
Amen

13

COOL MOTHERS

This is the genealogy of Jesus the Messiah the son of David,
the son of Abraham.
Matthew 1:1

The women mentioned in Christ's bloodline in Matthew Chapter 1 may seem a bit controversial to those on the outside peeping in. But in the eyes of God, they were perfect. There were five mothers specifically mentioned.

1. Tamar
This is not Tamar the raped daughter of King David, but Tamar who was married to a man named Er. But when Er died, it was customary for his brother to ensure she gave birth to a male in the bloodline. Er's brother refused and the father of Er lied to her, promising her an opportunity with Er's other younger brother. After Tamar realized she'd been lied to, she tricked her father-in-law Judah (as in the tribes of Judah) into sleeping with her by posing as a prostitute and she became pregnant with twins.

2. Rahab
Rahab was a well-known prostitute that protected the Israelite spies that came into her land. As a result of her protection, she and her family were saved. Consequently, she gave birth to a man named Boaz, who eventually married a woman named Ruth.

3. Ruth
Ruth was a widow who'd become so fond of her mother-in-law that she refused to return home to her own people when her husband passed away. Instead, she went to the land of her

mother-in-law and vowed to serve the God of her mother-in-law. She eventually went to work for, perhaps seduced (one night as she snuck into his room), and married a distant relative of her mother-in-law named Boaz, and gave birth to a man named Obed, who was the father of Jesse, father of King David.

4. Bathsheba

Bathsheba is also known as Uriah's wife, as when King David met her, she was bathing on a rooftop and he summoned her despite being well aware she was married. They conceived a child that did not live, but later conceived another (after David had her husband murdered and married her). The second child's name was Solomon and he went on to become a wise and wealthy king that fathered Rehoboam.

5. Mary

Mary was a young virgin engaged to the man of her dreams. But before they could marry, she is impregnated by the Holy Spirit and her reputation as a virtuous woman is tainted by gossip and whispers. Her fiance marries her despite her pregnancy and Jesus, the Messiah is born.

God will often use the foolish to confound the wise. These mothers were not those who would traditionally be characterized as "Proverbs 31" women. Instead, they were women who had people whispering about them behind their backs, fingers pointed at them as they walked down the street, poor treatment when they went in public for every day services, and worst of all, the backstabbing disrespect and gaslighting of their immediate families.

These were women who were forced to be strong in the face of adversity that they may accomplish the ultimate will of God to bring into life, the Savior of the world. These women weren't considered worthy of distinction, mention, or respect until the moment of Christ's glory arrived. Now each of them are etched in the legacy of Christ.

To receive the gift of salvation that leads to eternal life, we must only confess and believe in our hearts that Christ died for us. But to gain access to an abundant life, filled with wisdom, stature, and honor, we must place God first and be about His business.

Most Gracious and Heavenly Father,

How precious are Your thoughts toward us, O God! How vast is the sum of them! (1) Every good gift and every perfect gift is from above, coming down from the Father of lights with whom there is no variation or shadow due to change. (2) Therefore, we are thankful in all circumstances, for this is God's will for us who belong to Christ Jesus. (3) Just as we received Christ Jesus as Lord, we continue to live in him, strengthened in the faith as we were taught, and overflowing with thankfulness. (4) We trust in the LORD with all our hearts, and do not lean on our own understanding. In all our ways we acknowledge him, and he will make straight our paths. (5) We will not be conformed to this world, but be transformed by the renewal of our minds, that by testing we may discern what is the will of God, what is good and acceptable and perfect. (6) And it is our prayer that our love may abound more and more, with knowledge and all discernment, so that we may approve what is excellent, and so be pure and blameless for the day of Christ. (7)

The Spirit of the Lord will rest on us—the Spirit of wisdom and of understanding, the Spirit of counsel and of might, the Spirit of the knowledge and fear of the Lord—and we will delight in the fear of the Lord. (8)

And our ears shall hear a word behind us, saying, "This is the way, walk in it," when we turn to the right or when we turn to the left. (61) For the Lord knows the plans he has for us, plans for welfare and not for evil, to give us a future and a hope. (62) For the foolishness of God is wiser than men, and the weakness of God is stronger than men. (63) The steps of a man are established by the Lord, when he delights in his way. (64) For still the vision awaits its appointed time; it hastens to the end—it will not lie. If it seems slow, wait for it; it will surely come; it will not delay. (65) Looking to Jesus, the founder and perfecter of our faith, who for the joy that was set before him endured the cross, despising the shame, and is seated at the right hand of the throne of God. (66)

In Jesus Name,
Amen

14

JUDGE CORRECTLY

"Whoever believes in me, as Scripture has said, rivers of living water will flow from within them."
John 7:38

Jesus was hated by many, including his siblings. They did not believe he was the Savior of the world and they taunted him for being a leader among the people. Yet when confronted by them, Jesus did not back down. Instead, he doubled down and told them the truth.

At the time, the Jewish leaders wanted to kill Jesus. His siblings were aware and they tried to convince Jesus to show himself because "no one who wants to become a public figure acts in secret." But rather than take their ill-intended advice, Jesus does go but secretly.

Jesus heard the whispering gossip of the Jewish leaders, the people for him, and the people not yet convinced.

Jesus waited for an opportune time to teach. When the time came, he stood before many and taught the scriptures he received from God, which impressed those who were doing the will of God, as one who taught with efficiency and grace. Many in the crowd hated to hear him speak of personal sacrifice, the law, and sin, so they called him demon-possessed and insisted that no one wanted to kill him. He compared that to those that sought him when he provided miracles and told them to judge correctly.

The whispering gossip among them continued as they tried to determine if Jesus was good or evil. Again, when confronted publicly about his identity, Jesus did not cower but spoke boldly before them and insisted that he was indeed the Son of God sent by God. He told them that soon he would leave them and they would not be able to join him. This caused more whispering and gossip to occur.

But he told those who were thirsty to learn more, to drink the knowledge, and if they believed, out of their bellies would flow rivers of living water, meaning the Holy Spirit.

Jesus was operating on the basis of Isaiah 58. He was speaking boldly to those who did not believe and who felt as though their authority usurped the authority of God. He called them out and dared them to honor God with their lives, not in vanity or for show, but in reality as one seeking a true relationship with God.

Isaiah 58 challenges the believer to consider his ways. It begins with God seeking the truth from the one who eagerly seeks to see God's hand but not his face. He describes their vain fasting as disrespectful, disgraceful, and disingenuous. So God tells them what type of fasting will get a real response from him - true sacrifice.

A believer that wishes to honor God will sacrifice their creativity, time, and resources to honor God (as opposed to themselves). They will free the oppressed, give to the poor, feed the hungry, and take care of family. They will not gossip about others, point fingers or speak maliciously. They will honor the Sabbath and keep it holy, forsaking their own personal desires, and find delightful joy in honoring God.

Honoring God causes a shift in behavior. A life filled with sacrifice mirrors God, who created us in His likeness. He sacrificed his only son that we may live a life of freedom from sin. Our thank you to him is to turn away from sin and appreciate the grace he has afforded us.

To receive the gift of salvation that leads to eternal life, we must only confess and believe in our hearts that Christ died for us. But to gain access to an abundant life, filled with wisdom, stature, and honor, we must place God first and be about His business.

Most Gracious and Heavenly Father,

How precious are Your thoughts toward us, O God! How vast is the sum of them! (1) Every good gift and every perfect gift is from above, coming down from the Father of lights with whom there is no variation or shadow due to change. (2) Therefore, we are thankful in all circumstances, for this is God's will for us who belong to Christ Jesus. (3) Just as we received Christ Jesus as Lord, we continue to live in him, strengthened in the faith as we were taught, and overflowing with thankfulness. (4) We trust in the LORD with all our hearts, and do not lean on our own understanding. In all our ways we acknowledge him, and he will make straight our paths. (5) We will not be conformed to this world, but be transformed by the renewal of our minds, that by testing we may discern what is the will of God, what is good and acceptable and perfect. (6) And it is our prayer that our love may abound more and more, with knowledge and all discernment, so that we may approve what is excellent, and so be pure and blameless for the day of Christ. (7)

The Spirit of the Lord will rest on us—the Spirit of wisdom and of understanding, the Spirit of counsel and of might, the Spirit of the knowledge and fear of the Lord—and we will delight in the fear of the Lord. (8)

If we do away with the yoke of oppression, with the pointing finger and malicious talk, and if we spend ourselves in behalf of the hungry and satisfy the needs of the oppressed, then our light will rise in the darkness, and our night will become like the noonday. The Lord will guide us always; he will satisfy our needs in a sun-scorched land and will strengthen our frame. We will be like a well-watered garden, like a spring whose waters never fail. Our people will rebuild the ancient ruins and will raise up the age-old foundations; we will be called Repairer of Broken Walls, Restorer of Streets with Dwellings. (67)

In Jesus Name,
Amen

15

THOSE THAT LOVE HIS NAME DWELL THERE

I am worn out calling for help; my throat is parched. My eyes fail, looking for my God. Those who hate me without reason outnumber the hairs of my head; many are my enemies without cause, those who seek to destroy me. I am forced to restore what I did not steal.

Psalm 69:3-4

Jehosophat was a king that honored God, but someone he honored, spent time with, and blessed betrayed him and tried to kill him.

God inhabits the praises of His people. (68) Where two or three are gathered in Jesus' name, he is there in the midst. (69) Our prayers are a fragrant offering to God. (70) God searches the earth seeking hearts that are committed toward Him. (71)

We, like God, do not desire to be in places where we are simply tolerated. We want to be where our love is appreciated and reciprocated. God created us in His likeness. God gave us hearts that bear the weight of emotion, minds to logically decipher intention, bodies to carry and support the thoughts and ideas he shares with us, and the Holy Spirit to show us the way we are to go.

The Holy Spirit awakens us when we are threatened. He warns us to be alert, aware, responsive and spiritually prepared. The thief comes to steal, kill, and destroy. These are the tell tale signs of the enemy at work. When we see destruction, or witness the murdering of others (physically or emotionally), or the manipulation, deception, and gaslighting of the enemy at work, we must stand with the full armor of God: faith, salvation, truth, peace, righteousness, and the sword of the Spirit.

The Lord was with Jehoshaphat because he followed the ways of his father David before him. He did not consult the Baals but sought the God of his father and followed his commands rather than the practices of Israel. The Lord established the kingdom under his control; and all Judah brought gifts to Jehoshaphat, so that he had great wealth and honor. His heart was devoted to the ways of the Lord; furthermore, he removed the high places and the Asherah poles from Judah.

2 Chronicles 17:3-6

King Jehosophat trusted God and always sought God. When he was summoned by his father-in-law to go to war, he made sure that the king sought a prophet of God. But the king hated God's prophets because they always spoke truth regardless of what was trending, socially acceptable, or desired. When the prophet of God declared intentional deception and destruction for the king, the king refused to believe him. Instead the prophet of God was publicly humiliated and sent to prison and the king adopted the message of more than 400 false prophets. When it became time for war, instead of wearing his royal garments, he sent Jehosophat into battle dressed as the only king. The enemy targeted Jehosophat but soon realized he was not the king they were searching for. Instead a random arrow, pierced between the breastplates of the king who hated to hear from God, killing him and leaving his kingdom without a king as the prophet of God had predicted.

We cannot live a life of willful sin, ignore the voice and desire of God day in and day out, only call on him when our back is against the wall, question his advice, and expect victory. A relationship with God helps us to recognize the enemy afar off. In relationship with God, we seek his face and his advice before making a decision. We do not allow our emotions to take control. We are obedient to his instruction despite what we feel. We show up and honor him with more than the fruit of our lips, but also through our actions and deeds. We don't try to manipulate or outsmart our enemy, we let God fight our battles. He is more than able.

God loves everyone. He loves the murderers, liars, pimps, drug-dealers, false prophets, sanctimonious hypocrites, thieves, and unbelievers. But none does he consider worse than an unbeliever. Everyone we consider to be evil and unholy have a chance of making it to heaven… if they only believe. But an unbeliever, has little to no hope… unless they choose to believe.

As ambassadors of Christ, we sacrifice that others may see God and seek Him. We sacrifice that others will develop a closer relationship with God. God is no respecter of persons, none of us are more important than another - God values us all.

His love extends beyond offense, it supercedes our personal pain and sees the big picture. Our fight is not against flesh and blood, it is against principalities of evil. There is a spiritual war and the sacrifice of Jesus Christ is the greatest example of what is required from each of us. Christ died that we may have an opportunity to develop a relationship with God without the ritualistic natural sacrifice of animals on an altar. Instead, all we have to do is confess, believe, and respond with gratitude, relationship, and respect which reaps repentance and obedience.

To receive the gift of salvation that leads to eternal life, we must only confess and believe in our hearts that Christ died for us. But to gain access to an abundant life, filled with wisdom, stature, and honor, we must place God first and be about His business.

Most Gracious and Heavenly Father,

How precious are Your thoughts toward us, O God! How vast is the sum of them! (1) Every good gift and every perfect gift is from above, coming down from the Father of lights with whom there is no variation or shadow due to change. (2) Therefore, we are thankful in all circumstances, for this is God's will for us who belong to Christ Jesus. (3) Just as we received Christ Jesus as Lord, we continue to live in him, strengthened in the faith as we were taught, and overflowing with thankfulness. (4) We trust in the LORD with all our hearts, and do not lean on our own understanding. In all our ways we acknowledge him, and he will make straight our paths. (5) We will not be conformed to this world, but be transformed by the renewal of our minds, that by testing we may discern what is the will of God, what is good and acceptable and perfect. (6) And it is our prayer that our love may abound more and more, with knowledge and all discernment, so that we may approve what is excellent, and so be pure and blameless for the day of Christ. (7)

The Spirit of the Lord will rest on us—the Spirit of wisdom and of understanding, the Spirit of counsel and of might, the Spirit of the knowledge and fear of the Lord—and we will delight in the fear of the Lord. (8)

We will praise you with the harp for your faithfulness, our God; we will sing praise to you with the lyre, Holy One of Israel. Our lips will shout for joy when we sing praise to you—we whom you have delivered. Our tongues will tell of your righteous acts all day long, for those who wanted to harm us have been put to shame and confusion. (72)

In Jesus Name,
Amen

16

UNBELIEVABLY BLESSED

"Often, too, the fair speech of friends entrusted with the administration of affairs has induced many placed in authority to become accomplices in the shedding of innocent blood, and has involved them in irreparable calamities by deceiving with malicious slander the sincere good will of rulers. This can be verified in the ancient stories that have been handed down to us, but more fully when you consider the wicked deeds perpetrated in your midst by the pestilential influence of those undeserving of authority. We must provide for the future, so as to render the kingdom undisturbed and peaceful for all people, taking advantage of changing conditions and always deciding matters coming to our attention with equitable treatment.

"For instance, Haman, son of Hammedatha, a Macedonian, certainly not of Persian blood, and very different from us in generosity, was hospitably received by us. He benefited so much from the good will we have toward all peoples that he was proclaimed 'our father,' before whom everyone was to bow down; and he attained a position second only to the royal throne. But, unable to control his arrogance, he strove to deprive us of kingdom and of life, and by weaving intricate webs of deceit he demanded the destruction of Mordecai, our savior and constant benefactor, and of Esther, our blameless royal consort, together with their whole nation. For by such measures he hoped to catch us defenseless and to transfer the rule of the Persians to the Macedonians. But we find that the Jews, who were doomed to extinction by this archcriminal, are not evildoers, but rather are governed by very just laws and are the children of the Most High, the living God of majesty, who has maintained the kingdom in a flourishing condition for us and for our forebears.

"You will do well, then, to ignore the letter sent by Haman, son of Hammedatha, for he who composed it has been impaled, together with his entire household, before the gates of Susa. Thus swiftly has God, who governs all, brought just punishment upon him.

"You shall exhibit a copy of this letter publicly in every place to certify that the Jews may follow their own laws and that you may help them on the day set for their ruin, the thirteenth day of the twelfth month, Adar, to defend themselves against those who attack them. For God, the ruler of all, has turned that day from one of destruction of the chosen people into one of joy for them.

Esther 8: Chapter E - NASB, Excerpt from a Copy of the Letter Sent to the Governors of 127 Provinces (From India to Ethiopia)

Mordecai served the King of Persia but devoted his life to God. He worshipped God in wholeness and truth, teaching his family to do the same. He trusted God no matter the circumstance. When faced with new tyrannical leadership in the kingdom, he was forced to make a difficult decision. He was forced to choose between God and what others perceived as success. He was forced to disrupt the pattern to do what everyone expected and chose to do what God commanded. This one choice impacted not only him, but also every Jewish person that lived in their region including his niece who was just crowned as their queen.

For Mordecai, that singular decision brought an immense amount of angst, disrespect, and daily ridicule amplified by gossip. He did not deserve it, but he did his best to navigate it by not changing the quality of service he provided to the kingdom. Instead, Mordecai determined himself to be his best at all times to the point of saving the king's life when men plotted to kill the king.

Mordecai's ability to navigate the emotional, political, and social landmines angered Haman. Haman wanted to see Mordecai fail. He even built a gallows to publicly display his defeat and destruction of Haman. He laughed and prided himself in showing Mordecai daily that he was nothing and unimportant.

Queen Esther, Mordecai's niece, was in a position of power, but she was nervous about using it to protect her people. It could result in her death. But Mordecai's faith assured him that whether she helped or not, he was safe with God. He explained as much to her.

Queen Esther had to arm herself spiritually before taking such a bold step. But she did and as a result, not only were the lives of her people spared, but by law they were given permission to destroy their enemies and take ownership of what belonged to them.

Haman, the enemy of Mordecai and the Jews was killed along with his family. All that he owned was given to Queen Esther. Mordecai was crowned as second in command to the kingdom.

To receive the gift of salvation that leads to eternal life, we must only confess and believe in our hearts that Christ died for us. But to gain access to an abundant life, filled with wisdom, stature, and honor, we must place God first and be about His business.

Most Gracious and Heavenly Father,

How precious are Your thoughts toward us, O God! How vast is the sum of them! (1) Every good gift and every perfect gift is from above, coming down from the Father of lights with whom there is no variation or shadow due to change. (2) Therefore, we are thankful in all circumstances, for this is God's will for us who belong to Christ Jesus. (3) Just as we received Christ Jesus as Lord, we continue to live in him, strengthened in the faith as we were taught, and overflowing with thankfulness. (4) We trust in the LORD with all our hearts, and do not lean on our own understanding. In all our ways we acknowledge him, and he will make straight our paths. (5) We will not be conformed to this world, but be transformed by the renewal of our minds, that by testing we may discern what is the will of God, what is good and acceptable and perfect. (6) And it is our prayer that our love may abound more and more, with knowledge and all discernment, so that we may approve what is excellent, and so be pure and blameless for the day of Christ. (7)

The Spirit of the Lord will rest on us—the Spirit of wisdom and of understanding, the Spirit of counsel and of might, the Spirit of the knowledge and fear of the Lord—and we will delight in the fear of the Lord. (8)

Do not be deceived: God cannot be mocked. A man reaps what he sows. Whoever sows to please their flesh, from the flesh will reap destruction; whoever sows to please the Spirit, from the Spirit will reap eternal life. Let us not become weary in doing good, for at the proper time we will reap a harvest if we do not give up. Therefore, as we have opportunity, let us do good to all people, especially to those who belong to the family of believers. (73)

In Jesus Name,
Amen

17

PRIORITIZING LOVE

So the sisters sent word to Jesus,
"Lord, the one you love is sick."
John 11:3

Lazarus, Martha, and Mary were siblings that Jesus would fellowship with while visiting Bethany. Jesus loved each of them. Mary had many friends, some who were devout Jews. Martha was attentive to detail, not as social, and focused on doing what she felt called to do.

While preaching the gospel across the country, Jesus received word that Lazarus fell sick. He arrived in Bethany a couple of days after Lazarus died.

Martha met Christ upon arrival. She was the first to tell him that if he were there, her brother would not have died. But she wouldn't be the only person to say that, it seemed to be the recurring message among all who mourned him. Christ immediately promised Martha that her brother would rise again. But Martha assumed he meant in the after life. But Jesus again reassured her that anyone who dies and believes in Him shall live.

Jesus then called for Mary, who at the time, was in her home being comforted by friends. When Jesus felt her sense of loss and sorrow, it was a great weight in his Spirit. When her friends soon joined, their sorrow amplified the weight he felt and Jesus began to cry as well. Some of the people were moved when they witnessed Jesus weep for the loss of Lazarus but others questioned his abilities.

They took Jesus to the tomb and rolled the stone away. A hush fell over the people as Martha began to object noting a bad smell would be emitted. But Jesus turned to her again and insisted she believe. Then he prayed.

"Father, I thank you that you have heard me. I knew that you always hear me, but I said this for the benefit of the people standing here, that they may believe that you sent me."

John 11:41-42

After Lazarus was resurrected, some of the friends of Mary went to share the news with the Pharisees who told the Sanhedrin, who held a meeting to discuss the growing love for Jesus.

Then one of them, named Caiaphas, who was high priest that year, spoke up, "You know nothing at all! You do not realize that it is better for you that one man die for the people than that the whole nation perish."

He did not say this on his own, but as high priest that year he prophesied that Jesus would die for the Jewish nation, and not only for that nation but also for the scattered children of God, to bring them together and make them one. So from that day on they plotted to take his life.

John 11:49-53

Lazarus' death and resurrection was orchestrated by God to bring about his larger purpose, the willful execution of Jesus Christ that in amplification, Jesus may bring Gentile and Jew together as one.

Jesus prioritized his love for all people over the comfort of Lazarus, Mary, and Martha, those he also loved. They were entrusted with an assignment that only God could assign. While their suffering was but for a moment, Christ was sacrificed once and for all that we may all benefit.

When we prioritize love, we may also have to sacrifice our comfort to save the life of another.

To receive the gift of salvation that leads to eternal life, we must only confess and believe in our hearts that Christ died for us. But to gain access to an abundant life, filled with wisdom, stature, and honor, we must place God first and be about His business.

Most Gracious and Heavenly Father,

How precious are Your thoughts toward us, O God! How vast is the sum of them! (1) Every good gift and every perfect gift is from above, coming down from the Father of lights with whom there is no variation or shadow due to change. (2) Therefore, we are thankful in all circumstances, for this is God's will for us who belong to Christ Jesus. (3) Just as we received Christ Jesus as Lord, we continue to live in him, strengthened in the faith as we were taught, and overflowing with thankfulness. (4) We trust in the LORD with all our hearts, and do not lean on our own understanding. In all our ways we acknowledge him, and he will make straight our paths. (5) We will not be conformed to this world, but be transformed by the renewal of our minds, that by testing we may discern what is the will of God, what is good and acceptable and perfect. (6) And it is our prayer that our love may abound more and more, with knowledge and all discernment, so that we may approve what is excellent, and so be pure and blameless for the day of Christ. (7)

The Spirit of the Lord will rest on us—the Spirit of wisdom and of understanding, the Spirit of counsel and of might, the Spirit of the knowledge and fear of the Lord—and we will delight in the fear of the Lord. (8)

Lord, as the Father has loved you, so have you loved us. Now we remain in your love. If we keep your commands, we will remain in your love, just as you have kept our Father's commands and remained in his love. You have told us this so that our joy may be in you and that our joy may be complete. You commanded this: Love each other as you have loved us. Greater love has no one than this: to lay down one's life for one's friends. We are your friends if we do what you command. You no longer call us servants, because a servant does not know his master's business. Instead, you have called us friends, for everything that you learned from our Father you have made known to us. We did not choose you, but you chose us and appointed us so that we might go and bear fruit—fruit that will last—and so that whatever we ask in your name the Father will give us. This is your command: Love each other. (74)

In Jesus Name,
Amen

18

THE BLESSING OF GENEROSITY SELFLESSNESS AND HOSPITALITY

So Abram said to Lot, "Let's not have any quarreling between you and me, or between your herders and mine, for we are close relatives. Is not the whole land before you? Let's part company. If you go to the left, I'll go to the right; if you go to the right, I'll go to the left."

Genesis 13:8-9

Have you ever heard the phrase, "The grass is not greener on the other side?" So many times, we believe we know what we want, only to get it, and realize it was not as pleasant as it seemed.

Abram (soon to become Abraham) and Lot were uncle and nephew. After they left Egypt, Abram was very wealthy, and Lot had a handsome amount of money as well. They each had so much, they could not live in the same area and were forced to separate. Abram knew that he was going to be abundantly blessed, so he allowed Lot to select where he wanted to live.

Lot chose the most beautiful and lush area he could find, the plain of the Jordan. In the Bible, it said the land was green and fertile like the Garden of Eden, and like the land of Egypt. This alone is an interesting fact because when we consider the Middle East, we do not see lush, rolling hills of green pastures. We tend to see dry land. But it is believed that because of the flood that Noah prepared for in the Bible, these lands were more than likely just as described by Lot.

The Bible identifies the plain of Jordan as the region between Succoth and Zarthan north of Jericho (1 Kings 7:46). This area along the Jordan River from the Sea of Galilee in the north to Zoar at the south end of the Dead Sea is described as well-watered, like a garden. Zoar was one of the five cities of the plain (Sodom, Gomorrah, Admah, Zeboiim, and Zoar) on the southeastern shore of the Dead Sea. It is likely that the higher terrain to the west and east of the plain of Jordan would have been even wetter, because the hills would have been cooler and would therefore have received more rainfall.

The description of a moist, fertile landscape in Abraham's day is in stark contrast to the dry, desert environment of the Jordan Valley that exists today. Only near springs and along the riparian boundary of the Jordan where modern irrigation is practiced are any trees and green vegetation evident. The rainfall in the Jordan Valley south of the Sea of Galilee is so sparse that practically no vegetation of any kind is possible without irrigation in the hot, desert environment. Yet, as late as 1,000 years after the Flood (~1500 B.C.), about the time the Israelites were to enter the Promised Land, Palestine was described as "a land flowing with milk and honey" (Exodus 33:3).

In addition to the biblical hints of a wetter climate in Israel during the time of Abraham and Moses, paleoclimatological evidence also indicates that the entire Middle East experienced more precipitation, had more vegetation, and lakes were fuller.

https://www.icr.org/article/well-watered-land-effects-genesis-flood

Abram gave Lot what he desired without argument. Soon, after Lot departed, God visited Abram. He told Abram to look around in every direction and that all that his eyes could see would eventually belong to he and his offspring. Then God told him to go and walk the breadth of the land. Abram built an altar of worship to God in that place.

Lot moved he and his family very near to Sodom, a community that espoused itself with evil and completely disregarded God and all that God desired. Lot did not know it, but because he chose the grass he thought was greener, he cursed all that he cared for - family and land.

The city of Sodom was a cursed land. From the outside looking in, it seemed like a great place to live, raise a family, and grow his investments. But the land was cursed because of the activities that took place within it. Local kings attacked the land and took captive several members of the community and all their possessions, including Lot and his family. When Abram found out, he, his allies and his servants went to rescue Lot and his family. They also recovered all of Lot's possessions.

For this, Abram was honored and blessed by the King of Salem, Melchezidek, who was also the priest of the Most High God to whom Abram gave the first tithe noted in the Bible, a tenth of everything (not just all he secured but all that he owned). Then Abram returned to the king of Sodom all that he'd secured in battle, every person and every item.

After, Abram became Abraham and was given the opportunity to start his family. As the Lord, blessed he and Sarah his wife with the news that their son would be born within the year, he also warned Abraham that he would destroy Sodom. Abraham pleaded for the life of his nephew and loved ones.

Lot and his family would be forced to leave Sodom, amid chaos and death. Lot's family would be saved as they were rushed by angels into safety, with clear instructions, "Flee. Do not stop. Do not look back. Go to the mountains." His wife, who could not bear to leave it all behind, the material wealth and lifestyle she'd adopted and loved, looked back and immediately turned into a pillar of salt.

Later, as Lot and his daughters lived alone in a cave on the mountainside, the daughters feared being barren their entire lives. The curse of Sodom followed them and caused his daughters to drug and rape Lot as he slept that they might become pregnant and have children. His daughters gave birth to two of the enemy nations of God's people - the Moabites and Ammonites. Moab would eventually lead Israel into the worship of Baal. Both the Ammonites and the Moabites hired Balaam to curse Israel as it journeyed toward the Promised Land and were thus forbidden to enter the Lord's assembly.

In the book of Ezekiel, chapter 16, Ezekiel shares a word from the Lord with Israel condemning their actions in recent years. Specifically, relating to Sodom he shares,

"Now this was the sin of your sister Sodom: She and her daughters were arrogant, overfed and unconcerned; they did not help the poor and needy. They were haughty and did detestable things before me. Therefore I did away with them as you have seen."

Ezekiel 16:49

Many have assumed that Sodom was destroyed for its lascivious sexual activities, but in scripture, God specifically states it was because they were selfish, greedy, and inhospitable. Ezekiel then adds,

"Bear your disgrace, for you have furnished some justification for your sisters. Because your sins were more vile than theirs, they appear more righteous than you. So then, be ashamed and bear your disgrace, for you have made your sisters appear righteous."

Ezekiel 16:52

When we read the stories of the Old Testament, God reveals the true nature of man. We can be selfish, greedy, and inhospitable leading to our own detriment. When we choose not to protect the most vulnerable among us, or help those who are in need, or ignore our own responsibilities to gain more increase we not only curse ourselves but we also curse all that is most important to us - our relationship with God, our families, our investments, and our self-esteem.

But when we choose like Abraham to sacrifice what seems

like the best, for a life of commitment to God (communing with God, worshipping God, obeying God, and giving what belongs to God back to him) we not only receive the gift of God's presence each day but we also become conduits of unconditional love and are endowed with supernatural abilities to save and honor others. This is also symbolic of the life of Christ, his purpose and tendered reality.

Jesus has blessed each of us with an opportunity to receive the generous gift of salvation, his selfless sacrifice of life, and an open invitation, to each of us as sinners saved by grace, into the beautifu kingdom of heaven.

To receive the gift of salvation that leads to eternal life, we must only confess and believe in our hearts that Christ died for us. But to gain access to an abundant life, filled with wisdom, stature, and honor, we must place God first and be about His business.

Most Gracious and Heavenly Father,

How precious are Your thoughts toward us, O God! How vast is the sum of them! (1) Every good gift and every perfect gift is from above, coming down from the Father of lights with whom there is no variation or shadow due to change. (2) Therefore, we are thankful in all circumstances, for this is God's will for us who belong to Christ Jesus. (3) Just as we received Christ Jesus as Lord, we continue to live in him, strengthened in the faith as we were taught, and overflowing with thankfulness. (4) We trust in the LORD with all our hearts, and do not lean on our own understanding. In all our ways we acknowledge him, and he will make straight our paths. (5) We will not be conformed to this world, but be transformed by the renewal of our minds, that by testing we may discern what is the will of God, what is good and acceptable and perfect. (6) And it is our prayer that our love may abound more and more, with knowledge and all discernment, so that we may approve what is excellent, and so be pure and blameless for the day of Christ. (7)

The Spirit of the Lord will rest on us—the Spirit of wisdom and of understanding, the Spirit of counsel and of might, the Spirit of the knowledge and fear of the Lord—and we will delight in the fear of the Lord. (8)

The end of all things is near. Therefore we are alert and of sober mind so that we may pray. Above all, we love each other deeply, because love covers over a multitude of sins. We offer hospitality to one another without grumbling. Each of us should use whatever gifts we have received to serve others, as faithful stewards of God's grace in its various forms. If anyone speaks, we should do so as one who speaks the very words of God. If anyone serves, we should do so with the strength God provides, so that in all things God may be praised through Jesus Christ. To him be the glory and the power for ever and ever. (75)

In Jesus Name,
Amen

19

THE GLORY OF THE LORD

And I heard a loud voice from the throne saying, "Look! God's dwelling place is now among the people, and he will dwell with them. They will be his people, and God himself will be with them and be their God. 'He will wipe every tear from their eyes. There will be no more death' or mourning or crying or pain, for the old order of things has passed away."

Revelation 21:3-4

One who is given the opportunity to live in a land that is plush, beautiful and pleasant is blessed. But to live a life without darkness is a dream come true.

In heaven, God promises to not only allow us access to the most palacious of atmospheres but he also promises peace and tranquility. Gone will be the days of dodging sketchy and ill-intended people whose purpose is to gain regardless of the harm they exact. Forever forbidden will be those who refuse to believe in God.

Instead, God's brilliance will be reflected in all we experience, from purity of action, to the clarity of stone that surrounds his people. Heaven will extend to earth and the brilliance of God will be among us. Nations will bask in the light of God, and the kings of the earth will bring their most precious gifts into it.

Those who are given the opportunity to experience the new heaven and the new earth will no longer experience pain, and there will be no more tears. Sexual monsters are not allowed. The arrogant who believe they can control life, witches and magicians, will not be present. Murderers, those who willfully and callously destroy men, and those who support them - the cowardly who watch without complaint, revelation, or a whisper will not be allowed entry. No none of those who cause pain, especially the vain, who lie to protect an image that does not exist will be given access.

At it's center is God, and his brilliance reflects his glory. Jesus is his lamp. They are surrounded by precious stones, pure and excellent, of the highest quality. There are no locked doors, security gates, or surveillance systems, for all who are given access are pure and reflect the glory of God.

Nothing impure will ever enter it, nor will anyone who does what is shameful or deceitful, but only those whose names are written in the Lamb's book of life.
Revelation 21:27

Yes, one who is given the opportunity to live in a land that is plush, beautiful and pleasant is blessed. To live a life without darkness is a dream come true.

To receive the gift of salvation that leads to eternal life, we must only confess and believe in our hearts that Christ died for us. But to gain access to an abundant life, filled with wisdom, stature, and honor, we must place God first and be about His business.

Most Gracious and Heavenly Father,

How precious are Your thoughts toward us, O God! How vast is the sum of them! (1) Every good gift and every perfect gift is from above, coming down from the Father of lights with whom there is no variation or shadow due to change. (2) Therefore, we are thankful in all circumstances, for this is God's will for us who belong to Christ Jesus. (3) Just as we received Christ Jesus as Lord, we continue to live in him, strengthened in the faith as we were taught, and overflowing with thankfulness. (4) We trust in the LORD with all our hearts, and do not lean on our own understanding. In all our ways we acknowledge him, and he will make straight our paths. (5) We will not be conformed to this world, but be transformed by the renewal of our minds, that by testing we may discern what is the will of God, what is good and acceptable and perfect. (6) And it is our prayer that our love may abound more and more, with knowledge and all discernment, so that we may approve what is excellent, and so be pure and blameless for the day of Christ. (7)

The Spirit of the Lord will rest on us—the Spirit of wisdom and of understanding, the Spirit of counsel and of might, the Spirit of the knowledge and fear of the Lord—and we will delight in the fear of the Lord. (8)

Who is like You among the gods, O Lord? Who is like You, majestic in holiness, awesome in praises, working wonders? (76) Yours, O Lord, is the greatness and the power and the glory and the victory and the majesty, for all that is in the heavens and in the earth is yours. Yours is the kingdom, O Lord, and you are exalted as head above all. (77) The heavens declare the glory of God, and the sky above proclaims his handiwork. (78) Lift up your heads, O gates! And be lifted up, O ancient doors, that the King of glory may come in. Who is this King of glory? The Lord, strong and mighty, the Lord, mighty in battle! (79) May the glory of the Lord endure forever; may the Lord rejoice in his works, who looks on the earth and it trembles, who touches the mountains and they smoke! (80) Not to us, O Lord, not to us, but to your name give glory, for the sake of your steadfast love and your faithfulness! (81)

In Jesus Name,
Amen

20

MISTAKEN IDENTITY

But David said to Abishai, "Don't destroy him! Who can lay a hand on the Lord's anointed and be guiltless? As surely as the Lord lives," he said, "the Lord himself will strike him, or his time will come and he will die, or he will go into battle and perish. But the Lord forbid that I should lay a hand on the Lord's anointed. Now get the spear and water jug that are near his head, and let's go."

I Samuel 26:9-11

Saul was without a doubt an enemy to David. In fact, he'd tried to kill David on several occassions. But David, gave honor where honor was due. Despite having the perfect opportunity to kill a dominant and determined king that doggedly chased him with an intent to kill, he decided to leave the battle to the Lord.

This why David was a man after God's own heart. He trusted God.

But David did allow Saul to know that he was there. He called out to the head of the army protecting Saul and spoke. What David said was profound.

"Here is the king's spear," David answered. "Let one of your young men come over and get it. The Lord rewards everyone for their righteousness and faithfulness. The Lord delivered you into my hands today, but I would not lay a hand on the Lord's anointed. As surely as I valued your life today, so may the Lord value my life and deliver me from all trouble."

I Samuel 26:22-24

We are children of the Most High God and we cannot

forget who we are. Offenses come and go. We cannot live a life without offense. But when someone is chasing us and are determined to see us fail, there is only one option. Turn it over to the Lord. Let God fight the battle.

To receive the gift of salvation that leads to eternal life, we must only confess and believe in our hearts that Christ died for us. But to gain access to an abundant life, filled with wisdom, stature, and honor, we must place God first and be about His business.

Most Gracious and Heavenly Father,

How precious are Your thoughts toward us, O God! How vast is the sum of them! (1) Every good gift and every perfect gift is from above, coming down from the Father of lights with whom there is no variation or shadow due to change. (2) Therefore, we are thankful in all circumstances, for this is God's will for us who belong to Christ Jesus. (3) Just as we received Christ Jesus as Lord, we continue to live in him, strengthened in the faith as we were taught, and overflowing with thankfulness. (4) We trust in the LORD with all our hearts, and do not lean on our own understanding. In all our ways we acknowledge him, and he will make straight our paths. (5) We will not be conformed to this world, but be transformed by the renewal of our minds, that by testing we may discern what is the will of God, what is good and acceptable and perfect. (6) And it is our prayer that our love may abound more and more, with knowledge and all discernment, so that we may approve what is excellent, and so be pure and blameless for the day of Christ. (7)

The Spirit of the Lord will rest on us—the Spirit of wisdom and of understanding, the Spirit of counsel and of might, the Spirit of the knowledge and fear of the Lord—and we will delight in the fear of the Lord. (8)

We do not need to fight in this battle. We are to stand firm, hold our position, and see the salvation of the Lord on our behalf. We are not afraid and are not dismayed. Tomorrow we will go out against them, and the Lord will be with us. (82) We shall not fear them, for it is the Lord our God who fights for us. (83) No weapon that is fashioned against us shall succeed, and we shall refute every tongue that rises against us in judgment. This is the heritage of the servants of the Lord and our vindication is from the Lord, declares the Lord. (84)

In Jesus Name,
Amen

21

ORDINANCE

Sing aloud to God our strength; shout for joy to the God of Jacob (Israel). Raise a song, sound the timbrel, the sweet sounding lyre with the harp. Blow the trumpet at the New Moon, at the full moon, on our feast day. For this is a statute for Israel, an ordinance of the God of Jacob.He established it for a testimony in Joseph when He went throughout the land of Egypt.

Psalm 81:1-4

Joseph was sold into slavery by his brothers. He was subjected to servitude in a foreign land. He was unjustly imprisoned for crimes he did not commit. Yet, God gave him the victory. In the same land where he was enslaved and unjustly imprisoned, those that laughed, taunted, and made fun of him were forced to watch him be elevated by God to second in command to Pharaoah. The same family who hated him and willfully sent him away was forced to beg him for food as they faced starvation.

Joseph had to become resilient as he suffered through a period of his life that was filled with immense pain and shame. Despite his consistent and faithful worship to God, hard work, and respect and kindness he provided to all, his survival depended upon the strength of God.

For this reason, it is stated in the Psalm, that we are to sing to God our strength and to shout for joy because it is God who sees all and recognizes our pain, who balances the scale and requires justice where it did not formally exist. This is an ordinance, a law, established as a testimony for the sake of Joseph, who went throughout the land of Egypt.

Our worship is mandated by God because it is he who is with us in every circumstance. Such as the air we breathe from the moment we are born, is the spirit of God with us at every moment of life. God sees us, he knows our condition, he understands our pain, and he is a God of justice. God will not be mocked for what a man reaps, he shall sow.

To receive the gift of salvation that leads to eternal life, we must only confess and believe in our hearts that Christ died for us. But to gain access to an abundant life, filled with wisdom, stature, and honor, we must place God first and be about His business.

Most Gracious and Heavenly Father,

How precious are Your thoughts toward us, O God! How vast is the sum of them! (1) Every good gift and every perfect gift is from above, coming down from the Father of lights with whom there is no variation or shadow due to change. (2) Therefore, we are thankful in all circumstances, for this is God's will for us who belong to Christ Jesus. (3) Just as we received Christ Jesus as Lord, we continue to live in him, strengthened in the faith as we were taught, and overflowing with thankfulness. (4) We trust in the LORD with all our hearts, and do not lean on our own understanding. In all our ways we acknowledge him, and he will make straight our paths. (5) We will not be conformed to this world, but be transformed by the renewal of our minds, that by testing we may discern what is the will of God, what is good and acceptable and perfect. (6) And it is our prayer that our love may abound more and more, with knowledge and all discernment, so that we may approve what is excellent, and so be pure and blameless for the day of Christ. (7)

The Spirit of the Lord will rest on us—the Spirit of wisdom and of understanding, the Spirit of counsel and of might, the Spirit of the knowledge and fear of the Lord—and we will delight in the fear of the Lord. (8)

Lord, you are our God; we will exalt you and praise your name, for in perfect faithfulness you have done wonderful things, things planned long ago. (85) Let everything that has breath praise the Lord. Praise the Lord. (86) God is spirit, and his worshipers must worship in the Spirit and in truth. (87) Those who hate the Lord would cringe before him, and their punishment would last forever. But we will be fed with the finest of wheat; with honey from the rock God would satisfy us. (88)

In Jesus Name,
Amen

22

YOU SHALL REAP
WHAT YOU SOW

Eliphaz falsely accused Job of sin but stated a truism:
"Those who plow iniquity and sow trouble reap the same."
Job 4:8

All too often, we compare our lives to the lives of others and wonder what we are doing wrong. We look into the mirror and wonder how we have become who we have become and are constantly wondering what others see when they see us.

But what is most important is for us to ponder what God sees when he sees us. Does he see a faithful servant that enjoys spending time with him? Does he see someone who is willing to sacrifice what they desire for the greater good of others? Does he see someone that will follow directions? Does he see someone that will say "thank you" and appreciate all of his gifts, provision, and protection? God knows us, intimately, whether we open ourselves to him or not. He created each of us and he recognizes the burdens, sorrows, joy, and hope we carry.

Sometimes we avoid the truth because it is too painful to face. Instead, we become angry or depressed (anger turned inward) and spiral. This is when praise becomes a sacrifice, obedience becomes arduous, and courtesy becomes strained. But when we shine a light in the darkness, face what is wrong head on, and push through, we can begin to see a light at the end of the tunnel.

Jesus taught about sowing and reaping. He shared how a

good seed sown in different ways can reap different results. This is true for the farmer as well. A farmer who plants a seed expects that crop to grow, but the conditions have to be right.

It is same for all things in life, but most especially the Word of God. Sometimes the land has to be tilled, or broken in that it can generate the best results.

Tilling is the practice of aerating the soil to permit moisture and air to permeate, allowing seeds to germinate, encouraging root growth, controlling weed growth, and integrating fertilizers into the soil. One field may be tilled multiple times before planting for different reasons.

Oregon State University - Tillage and Cultivation | College of Agricultural Sciences

We must have an open heart to receive the Word of God, a life subjected to the will of God that the Holy Spirit may guide us, and a soul that is trained by the consistent and continual worship of God that it may not resist the will of God when seasons of darkness shadow our way.

The truth is we will all face dark times. But it is only by the grace of God that we are able navigate those times according to his will. In this way, God is tilling our soil.

Adversity can be good, disruption can be healthy, and discomfort has its purpose. In the moment, our pain is amplified and even after the moment passes, it echoes for a time. But in the echo, we see what we could not in the moment. In the echo, we realize our missteps.

What we reap, we sow. How we sow effects the outcome. Jesus sacrificed his life unto death, that we may reap life, in fact, abundant life. He lived a perfect life, that our lives, scattered with sin, could be washed clean. He died that we may live.

To receive the gift of salvation that leads to eternal life, we must only confess and believe in our hearts that Christ died for us. But to gain access to an abundant life, filled with

wisdom, stature, and honor, we must place God first and be about His business.

Most Gracious and Heavenly Father,

How precious are Your thoughts toward us, O God! How vast is the sum of them! (1) Every good gift and every perfect gift is from above, coming down from the Father of lights with whom there is no variation or shadow due to change. (2) Therefore, we are thankful in all circumstances, for this is God's will for us who belong to Christ Jesus. (3) Just as we received Christ Jesus as Lord, we continue to live in him, strengthened in the faith as we were taught, and overflowing with thankfulness. (4) We trust in the LORD with all our hearts, and do not lean on our own understanding. In all our ways we acknowledge him, and he will make straight our paths. (5) We will not be conformed to this world, but be transformed by the renewal of our minds, that by testing we may discern what is the will of God, what is good and acceptable and perfect. (6) And it is our prayer that our love may abound more and more, with knowledge and all discernment, so that we may approve what is excellent, and so be pure and blameless for the day of Christ. (7)

The Spirit of the Lord will rest on us—the Spirit of wisdom and of understanding, the Spirit of counsel and of might, the Spirit of the knowledge and fear of the Lord—and we will delight in the fear of the Lord. (8)

We will sow our seed in the morning, and at evening let our hands not be idle, for we do not know which will succeed, whether this or that, or whether both will do equally well. (89) Whoever sows to please their flesh, from the flesh will reap destruction; whoever sows to please the Spirit, from the Spirit will reap eternal life. (90) But the seed on good soil stands for those with a noble and good heart, who hear the word, retain it, and by persevering produce a crop. (91) Isaac planted crops in that land and the same year reaped a hundredfold, because the LORD blessed him. (92) Whoever sows sparingly will also reap sparingly, and whoever sows generously will also reap generously. We should give what we have decided in our heart to give, not reluctantly or under compulsion, for God loves a cheerful giver. And God is able to bless us abundantly, so that in all things at all times, having all that we need, we will abound in every good work. As it is written: "They have freely scattered their gifts to the poor; their righteousness endures forever." God who supplies seed to the sower and bread for food will also supply and increase our store of seed and will enlarge the harvest of our righteousness. We will be enriched in every way so that we can be generous on every occasion, and our generosity will result in thanksgiving to God. This service that we perform is not only supplying the needs of the Lord's people but is also overflowing in many expressions of thanks to God. Because of the service by which we have proved ourselves, others will praise God for the obedience that accompanies our confession of the gospel of Christ, and for our generosity in sharing with them and with everyone else. And in their prayers for us their hearts will go out to us, because of the surpassing grace God has given us. Thanks be to God for his indescribable gift! (93)

In Jesus Name,
Amen

23

PATIENT CONFIDENCE AND THE NECESSITY OF BOLDNESS

Now Elisha was sitting in his house,
and the elders were sitting with him.
The king sent a messenger ahead, but before he arrived,
Elisha said to the elders, "Don't you see how this murderer is sending
someone to cut off my head? Look, when the messenger comes, shut
the door and hold it shut against him. Is not the sound of his master's
footsteps behind him?"

While he was still talking to them, the messenger came down to him.

The king said, "This disaster is from the Lord.
Why should I wait for the Lord any longer?"
2 Kings 6:32-33

Anyone that is willing to do and say what God commands requires three distinct characteristics: patience, confidence, and boldness. Every successful and victorious person in the Bible has exemplified these three traits. Anger, disgruntledness, disrespect and disagreements do not honor God and they do not win over those you have been assigned to share the love of God with. But when your back is against the wall and others are depending on you, it is difficult not to lose your patience, confidence and boldness.

The people of Israel's kingdom were starving, so much so that a woman had just told the king that she and her friend had eaten her son the night before to survive. It is no wonder he was at his wit's end. But Elijah knew that God was faithful and instead of responding in fear when his life was threatened, he prophesied that within twenty-four hours the famine would be over and... It was. But not before a lot of really bad and uncomfortable things happened in the kingdom.

Walking with God does not mean that we will be comfortable or even like what we are called to do. It does mean that as his children, we know that God is trustworthy and deserves our praise.

David was not well-loved by his family. In fact, his father did not even believe he could be anointed as king. When the prophet Samuel arrived to anoint a member of David's family, his father left him alone to tend the sheep in the fields while calling all of his brothers into the home in hopes that one of them would be anointed. But God saw David and he loved David. He thought he was worthy to be a king and not just any king. David was part of the bloodline of Jesus.

Many of us spend our lives feeling and being overlooked by those we wish could or would acknowledge our value and worth. We work hard, give and love only to be treated as though we are not important and do not matter.

We have to have faith that God sees us and he knows how we feel. We cannot allow our circumstances to dictate our behavior. Instead we have to buckle down and wait on God. We have to hold our heads high and walk in boldness. We have to follow his every command even when it does not make sense to anyone around us. We must be willing to build our arks in the middle of the drought.

The boldness is necessary. We do not achieve our goals if we just wait and have hope. Faith without works is dead. Our faith requires it be activated and predicated by actions that are senseless to those on the outside looking in. We have to be willing to write books that aren't selling. Pay staff without profits. Take a job that doesn't pay more and uses more of our time. Work with people who disrespect us and take advantage of our kindness. Why? Because God says to do it. Not because it makes sense or feels good.

We've seen these traits in many prophets and powerful men and women of God - Elijah, Jeremiah, Isaiah, Daniel, even Joseph. Trusting God requires that we stand in faith in the face of opposition and believe him just enough to take a bold action. Say no when others want us to say yes. Ask for more when others would simply accept what is offered. Pray and speak about our faith when people just want to talk about movies, music, money, sports, sex, politics, and power. It is our job to prepare a way for the Lord to travel. The only way we can do that is if we meditate on his Word and seek him day and night.

To receive the gift of salvation that leads to eternal life, we must only confess and believe in our hearts that Christ died for us. But to gain access to an abundant life, filled with wisdom, stature, and honor, we must place God first and be about His business.

Most Gracious and Heavenly Father,

How precious are Your thoughts toward us, O God! How vast is the sum of them! (1) Every good gift and every perfect gift is from above, coming down from the Father of lights with whom there is no variation or shadow due to change. (2) Therefore, we are thankful in all circumstances, for this is God's will for us who belong to Christ Jesus. (3) Just as we received Christ Jesus as Lord, we continue to live in him, strengthened in the faith as we were taught, and overflowing with thankfulness. (4) We trust in the LORD with all our hearts, and do not lean on our own understanding. In all our ways we acknowledge him, and he will make straight our paths. (5) We will not be conformed to this world, but be transformed by the renewal of our minds, that by testing we may discern what is the will of God, what is good and acceptable and perfect. (6) And it is our prayer that our love may abound more and more, with knowledge and all discernment, so that we may approve what is excellent, and so be pure and blameless for the day of Christ. (7)

The Spirit of the Lord will rest on us—the Spirit of wisdom and of understanding, the Spirit of counsel and of might, the Spirit of the knowledge and fear of the Lord—and we will delight in the fear of the Lord. (8)

The Lord is our light and our salvation. Whom shall we fear? The Lord is the stronghold of our life, of whom shall we be afraid? (94) If God is for us, who can be against us? He who did not spare his own Son, but gave him up for us all—how will he not also, along with him, graciously give us all things? (95) The wicked flee when no one pursues, but the righteous are like a lion. (96) Let us then with confidence draw near to the throne of grace, that we may receive mercy and find grace to help in time of need. (97) Since we have such a hope, we are very bold.(98)

In Jesus Name,
Amen

24

PRIVILEGED VULNERABILITIES

"See, I lay in Zion a stone that causes people to stumble and a rock that makes them fall, and the one who believes in him will never be put to shame."

Romans 9:33

Life is not fair, it is not just, and the scales don't always balance.

God is intentional. He sets one up and allows another to fall beneath. He hardens the heart of Pharoah that Moses may deliver. He strengthens the confidence of David while weakening the defense of Saul. He quiets the resolute and beautiful innocence of Tamar to reveal the brazen and disruptive nature of Absalom. He allows Adam to fall that Christ may rise.

The Israelites received the promise by birth and nature, but those who believe in Christ receive the promise by faith. It is faith that determines the destination of those who are called, not birthright or race. Privileged vulnerabilities are had by those who assume that their stature is what elevates them, but this elevation is predetermined by God and is spirit-filled.

As it was with Sarah who gave birth to Isaac well after she or Abraham were physically able to conceive, the promise of God defies the finite ability of humanity and arises from the Lord's supernatural desire and purpose. The same is witnessed in the birth of the prophet Samuel, and the prophecy of Joseph born to a barren and hopeless Rebecca, the pre-determined destinies of Jacob and Esau before either was born… and the blessing of Ephraim over his brother Manasseh despite their birth order.

When Joseph saw his father placing his right hand on Ephraim's head he was displeased; so he took hold of his father's hand to move it from Ephraim's head to Manasseh's head. Joseph said to him, "No, my father, this one is the firstborn; put your right hand on his head."

But his father refused and said, "I know, my son, I know. He too will become a people, and he too will become great. Nevertheless, his younger brother will be greater than he, and his descendants will become a group of nations." He blessed them that day and said,

"In your name will Israel pronounce this blessing: 'May God make you like Ephraim and Manasseh.'"

So he put Ephraim ahead of Manasseh.

Genesis 48:17-20

Regardless of the predetermined condition or position God has called us to, we are to bless the Lord at all times. His praise belongs in our hearts and should flow from our lips. God does not make mistakes. He will not allow those who believe, trust, and worship Him to be brought to a position of shame.

To receive the gift of salvation that leads to eternal life, we must only confess and believe in our hearts that Christ died for us. But to gain access to an abundant life, filled with wisdom, stature, and honor, we must place God first and be about His business.

Most Gracious and Heavenly Father,

How precious are Your thoughts toward us, O God! How vast is the sum of them! (1) Every good gift and every perfect gift is from above, coming down from the Father of lights with whom there is no variation or shadow due to change. (2) Therefore, we are thankful in all circumstances, for this is God's will for us who belong to Christ Jesus. (3) Just as we received Christ Jesus as Lord, we continue to live in him, strengthened in the faith as we were taught, and overflowing with thankfulness. (4) We trust in the LORD with all our hearts, and do not lean on our own understanding. In all our ways we acknowledge him, and he will make straight our paths. (5) We will not be conformed to this world, but be transformed by the renewal of our minds, that by testing we may discern what is the will of God, what is good and acceptable and perfect. (6) And it is our prayer that our love may abound more and more, with knowledge and all discernment, so that we may approve what is excellent, and so be pure and blameless for the day of Christ. (7)

The Spirit of the Lord will rest on us—the Spirit of wisdom and of understanding, the Spirit of counsel and of might, the Spirit of the knowledge and fear of the Lord—and we will delight in the fear of the Lord. (8)

In love, you predestined us for adoption to yourself as children through Christ. (99) For to all who did receive him, who believed in his name, he gave the right to become children of God. Who were born, not of blood nor of the will of the flesh nor of the will of man, but of God. (100) For all who are led by the Spirit of God are sons of God. For we did not receive the spirit of slavery to fall back into fear, but we have received the Spirit of adoption as sons, by whom we cry, "Abba! Father!" The Spirit himself bears witness with our spirit that we are children of God, and if children, then heirs—heirs of God and fellow heirs with Christ, provided we suffer with him in order that we may also be glorified with him. (101)

In Jesus Name,
Amen

25

COURAGE
STRENGTH
HONOR
AND SACRIFICE

Brothers and sisters, choose seven men from among you who are known to be full of the Spirit and wisdom. We will turn this responsibility over to them and will give our attention to prayer and the ministry of the word.

——-------

Now Stephen, a man full of God's grace and power, performed great wonders and signs among the people.

Acts 6:3-4,8

Speaking truth to power is not for the faint of heart. Standing strong in the face of opposition requires courage. Trusting God in moments of unrest and uncertainty requires an abundance of faith. In every season, at every moment, we must lean on the unrelenting power of the Holy Spirit.

Have you ever heard of 'Meals on Wheels'? It is a program designed to ensure that the elderly and shut in receive hot, fresh, food daily. The disciples were basically performing this action but felt their time was best used in sharing the Gospel of Jesus Christ among those in the community. So they found a group of young men, with the intention of finding men that were filled with the Holy Spirit, to assist them in feeding the widows within their community.

Stephen was selected because he was a believer that was filled with the Holy Spirit. But because Stephen was effective in his ministry, studied the Word of God, and could answer any question about the gospel with the wisdom of the Holy Spirit he was hated by those who challenged his beliefs.

Then they secretly persuaded some men to say, "We have heard Stephen speak blasphemous words against Moses and against God."

Acts 6:11

Stephen, an innocent man doing the will of God, as requested by his elders was snatched by religious zealots and presented to the Jewish court. He was accused of disrespecting the holy place and the law. But those who were to judge him could only see the face of an angel.

As his trial progressed, Stephen witnessed to them about the story of Jesus Christ. He began with their Jewish history and ended with a powerful conviction about his crucifixion. For this, they stoned Stephen. They literally covered their ears, snatched him, dragged him from the city and threw rocks at him.

Stephen was selected to serve because of his faith and his connection to the Holy Spirit. But it was this very distinctive trait that caused him to be persecuted unto death before his peers. I strongly believe that Stephen never imagined that an opportunity and position of honor would lead to a public death being taunted by those he respected for many years.

Prophets live a life of honor to bring glory to God. Daniel faced lions, Jeremiah was placed in a miry pit with only bread and water, Elijah was threatened repeatedly by many, Stephen was stoned, and Jesus was crucified. Walking with God does not mean that you will not be attacked, disrespected, mistreated, or even crucified by man. But God is faithful, the record of Jesus, the account of Stephen, and every prophet before them is a record of honor, respect, and courage. Their legacy is one fueled by faith and carried on the lips of believers. Their ability to overcome opposition with their head held high, despite a temporary end is what distinguishes each as pillars in the great hall of faith, with Jesus at the head of them all. Jesus Christ is the King of Kings, the Lord of Lords, and Our Savior. The chastisement of our peace is upon him.

Let each of us run on that we may see what the end will be.

To receive the gift of salvation that leads to eternal life, we must only confess and believe in our hearts that Christ died for us. But to gain access to an abundant life, filled with wisdom, stature, and honor, we must place God first and be about His business.

Most Gracious and Heavenly Father,

How precious are Your thoughts toward us, O God! How vast is the sum of them! (1) Every good gift and every perfect gift is from above, coming down from the Father of lights with whom there is no variation or shadow due to change. (2) Therefore, we are thankful in all circumstances, for this is God's will for us who belong to Christ Jesus. (3) Just as we received Christ Jesus as Lord, we continue to live in him, strengthened in the faith as we were taught, and overflowing with thankfulness. (4) We trust in the LORD with all our hearts, and do not lean on our own understanding. In all our ways we acknowledge him, and he will make straight our paths. (5) We will not be conformed to this world, but be transformed by the renewal of our minds, that by testing we may discern what is the will of God, what is good and acceptable and perfect. (6) And it is our prayer that our love may abound more and more, with knowledge and all discernment, so that we may approve what is excellent, and so be pure and blameless for the day of Christ. (7)

The Spirit of the Lord will rest on us—the Spirit of wisdom and of understanding, the Spirit of counsel and of might, the Spirit of the knowledge and fear of the Lord—and we will delight in the fear of the Lord. (8)

Even though we walk through the valley of the shadow of death, we will fear no evil, for you are with us; your rod and your staff, they comfort us. (102) Peace you leave with us; your peace you give to us. Not as the world gives do you give to us. Therefore, we will not allow our hearts be troubled or afraid. (103) When we are afraid, we put our trust in you. In God, whose word we praise, in God we trust; we shall not be afraid. What can flesh do to us? (104) For you are with us in weakness and in fear and much trembling. (105) Finally, we are strong in the Lord and in the strength of his might. (106) When we go out to battle against our enemies and we see horses and chariots and people larger than us, we will not be afraid because God is with us - the same God that brought us out of Egypt. (107)

In Jesus Name,
Amen

26

LET GOD DO IT

Come, all you who are thirsty, come to the waters;
and you who have no money, come, buy and eat!
Come, buy wine and milk without money and without cost.

Isaiah 55:1

Every day we strive to become wiser, stronger, faster, and simply better. But God has all wisdom, all power, all of time and control over all things. So why are we trying to do what God has already done?

What if we dared to let go of what we think is the path to greatness, and simply allowed God to lead us? What if instead of spending time doing things we think will elevate us, we prioritized spending time with God, reading the Word, confessing our praise, and offering continuous prayer?

We are to be about His business. But we can't do that unless we know what God desires. His desires are outlined in His Word.

Let the wicked forsake his way and the evil man his thoughts.
Let him turn to the LORD, and he will have mercy on him,
and to our God, for he will freely pardon.

Isaiah 55:7

God doesn't hold grudges. Hell is for those who don't believe in God. Only unbelief will allow us to continue down a path that is unhealthy for ourselves and others. God can't save anyone who doesn't believe that their sins are forgiven (no matter how heinous they are), and doesn't believe that God can heal and make whole.

God's word is bond.

"As the heavens are higher than the earth, so are my ways higher than your ways and my thoughts than your thoughts. As the rain and the snow come down from heaven, and do not return to it without watering the earth and making it bud and flourish, so that it yields seed for the sower and bread for the eater, so is my word that goes out from my mouth: It will not return to me empty, but will accomplish what I desire and achieve the purpose for which I sent it. You will go out in joy and be led forth in peace; the mountains and hills will burst into song before you, and all the trees of the field will clap their hands.

Instead of the thornbush will grow the pine tree, and instead of briers the myrtle will grow. This will be for the LORD's renown, for an everlasting sign, which will not be destroyed."

Isaiah 55:9-13

The Lord's desire is to bless us, at no cost to us. All we have to do is walk with Him and believe what he says. Doors will open that no man can shut. Every blessing promised in his Word belongs to us. We will be able to request the company of nations that we don't know and they will run to us. We are witnesses of God's glory, leaders among men, distinguished and respected. Our lives are walking testimonies of God's goodness. Our actions are honored because we walk in obedience to the Most High. Our presence is desired because God's glory can shine brightly before men.

This is the art of debt-free living, which is only established by a trust in God that assures us that when we prioritize His business, everything we hope for and desire will be. All we have to do is let go and let God.

To receive the gift of salvation that leads to eternal life, we must only confess and believe in our hearts that Christ died for us. But to gain access to an abundant life, filled with wisdom, stature, and honor, we must place God first and be about His business.

Most Gracious and Heavenly Father,

How precious are Your thoughts toward us, O God! How vast is the sum of them! (1) Every good gift and every perfect gift is from above, coming down from the Father of lights with whom there is no variation or shadow due to change. (2) Therefore, we are thankful in all circumstances, for this is God's will for us who belong to Christ Jesus. (3) Just as we received Christ Jesus as Lord, we continue to live in him, strengthened in the faith as we were taught, and overflowing with thankfulness. (4) We trust in the LORD with all our hearts, and do not lean on our own understanding. In all our ways we acknowledge him, and he will make straight our paths. (5) We will not be conformed to this world, but be transformed by the renewal of our minds, that by testing we may discern what is the will of God, what is good and acceptable and perfect. (6) And it is our prayer that our love may abound more and more, with knowledge and all discernment, so that we may approve what is excellent, and so be pure and blameless for the day of Christ. (7)

The Spirit of the Lord will rest on us—the Spirit of wisdom and of understanding, the Spirit of counsel and of might, the Spirit of the knowledge and fear of the Lord—and we will delight in the fear of the Lord. (8)

And we know that in all things God works for the good of those who love him, who[a] have been called according to his purpose. (108) Therefore we are still, and know that you are God. (109) We do not consider ourselves yet to have taken hold of it. But one thing we do: forget what is behind and straining toward what is ahead, we press on toward the goal to win the prize for which God has called me heavenward in Christ Jesus. (110) Now to him who is able to do immeasurably more than all we ask or imagine, according to his power that is at work within us. Unto him be glory in the church by Christ Jesus throughout all ages, world without end. (111)

In Jesus Name,
Amen

27

THE LORD IS OUR STRENGTH

*You that love the Lord, hate evil: he preserves the souls of his saints;
he delivers them out of the hand of the wicked. Light is sown for the
righteous, and gladness for the upright in heart.*

Psalm 97:10-11

Pressure can make us become who we hate to be. Anger
and resentment, malice and unrest can bubble under the surface
of someone who feels like justice is out of their reach. It also
keeps us from discovering our purpose in Christ daily.

Every day that we wake up, God desires that we move in
alignment with his will. We are to stay in the flow of the Holy
Spirit. By remaining in his flow, we can experience his light, his
love, and his kindness.

For this reason, we must hate evil. By hating evil, we assure
we are not participants in evil activities. We do not wallow in sin,
or bathe and bask in the tenets of sin. Instead, we run from sinful
activities, and we stray away from opportunities that present
themselves as secret sins.

*Elijah was afraid and ran for his life. When he came to Beersheba in
Judah, he left his servant there, while he himself went a day's journey
into the wilderness. He came to a broom bush, sat down under it and
prayed that he might die. "I have had enough, Lord," he said.
"Take my life; I am no better than my ancestors." Then he lay down
under the bush and fell asleep.*

I Kings 19:4-5

Sheep are prey animals; their only defense is to run. But

with Jesus as our shepherd, we are not simply running blindly -
we are running directly to him. We seek rest beneath the shadow
of his wings, we embrace his mercy and his grace. We recognize
his sovereignty and beg his forgiveness when we have fallen and
are unable to lift ourselves back up. We seek him while he may be
found that he can help us in our time of trouble.

Elijah had just defeated the enemy in a mighty way -
removing the influence of hundreds of false prophets with the
entire community of Israelites as witness. In response, his life
was threatened by the leader of the false prophets, an evil woman
named Jezebel, known for killing the prophets of God. Jezebel
vowed to have Elijah murdered within 24-hours. Elijah was weary
from battle and feared for his life. He felt he'd reached the end of
his abilities and was ready to give up.

Soon after he'd fallen asleep, Elijah was awakened by an
angel who insisted that he get up and eat. After which he traveled
40 days and nights to Mount Horeb. (Now Elijah, who before
the battle with the false prophets had spent an entire season of
drought in isolation and hiding found himself once again, alone
and on a mountain).

God asked him, "What are you doing here?"

This is a question that often echoes in our minds in times
of confusion, chaos, and unrest.

Elijah explained to God that he felt as though he was
fighting an uphill battle alone.

God then showed Elijah that he would never be found in
the chaos of life, (hurricanes, earthquakes and fires) but instead,
God was the still, small voice that guided Elijah every day. Elijah
also recognized this, as he ignored the chaos outside the cave, but
when he heard God whisper, he exited the cave to see what God
would say.

God told Elijah to return by the way he came. He instructed Elijah to gift the anointing to others (Jehu, Elisha, & Hazael) whom God had blessed to be a help to him. Jehu, the anointed king of Israel, killed Jezebel, the woman who vowed to take Elijah's life. Elisha was anointed to carry on the legacy of Elijah and become a prophet to many. Elijah no longer felt alone on the battlefield.

Pressure can cause us to question God's intentions toward us. Even when we are victorious in the toughest of battles, we can find ourselves facing new enemies that seem too strong for us. It is in these moments, moments when we are tired, disgruntled, uncertain and unsure that we must lean on the presence of God. We must confess to God what is true in our hearts and pray that God will carry us through. We must trust the Lord in all circumstances.

But even when we trust God in every situation, we find ourselves in uncomfortable places and uncomfortable positions. Jesus was rejected by the world, he was a perfect and sinless man, yet hated by many and treated with disrespect - but he trusted God. He trusted that the God he communed with was honest and true. He believed that the Word was unable to fail him and while outwardly he suffered at the hands of godless men, inwardly he won a battle that no other could win.

When our way gets tough, and the road gets lonely, we do not have to fret, worry, or doubt. We can run to Jesus and let him fight the battle. We are tasked with strengthening the inward man as we face opposition and challenges that only God can see us through. The Lord is our strength.

To receive the gift of salvation that leads to eternal life, we must only confess and believe in our hearts that Christ died for us. But to gain access to an abundant life, filled with wisdom, stature, and honor, we must place God first and be about His business.

Most Gracious and Heavenly Father,

How precious are Your thoughts toward us, O God! How vast is the sum of them! (1) Every good gift and every perfect gift is from above, coming down from the Father of lights with whom there is no variation or shadow due to change. (2) Therefore, we are thankful in all circumstances, for this is God's will for us who belong to Christ Jesus. (3) Just as we received Christ Jesus as Lord, we continue to live in him, strengthened in the faith as we were taught, and overflowing with thankfulness. (4) We trust in the LORD with all our hearts, and do not lean on our own understanding. In all our ways we acknowledge him, and he will make straight our paths. (5) We will not be conformed to this world, but be transformed by the renewal of our minds, that by testing we may discern what is the will of God, what is good and acceptable and perfect. (6) And it is our prayer that our love may abound more and more, with knowledge and all discernment, so that we may approve what is excellent, and so be pure and blameless for the day of Christ. (7)

The Spirit of the Lord will rest on us—the Spirit of wisdom and of understanding, the Spirit of counsel and of might, the Spirit of the knowledge and fear of the Lord—and we will delight in the fear of the Lord. (8)

God is our refuge and strength, an ever-present help in trouble. Therefore we will not fear, though the earth give way and the mountains fall into the heart of the sea, though its waters roar and foam and the mountains quake with their surging. There is a river whose streams make glad the city of God, the holy place where the Most High dwells. God is within her, she will not fall; God will help her at break of day. Nations are in uproar, kingdoms fall; he lifts his voice, the earth melts. The Lord Almighty is with us; the God of Jacob is our fortress. Come and see what the Lord has done, the desolations he has brought on the earth. He makes wars cease to the ends of the earth. He breaks the bow and shatters the spear; he burns the shields with fire. He says, "Be still, and know that I am God; I will be exalted among the nations, I will be exalted in the earth." The Lord Almighty is with us; the God of Jacob is our fortress.

In Jesus Name,
Amen

28

EXCEEDING EXPECTATIONS

*In the midst of a very severe trial, their overflowing joy and their
extreme poverty welled up in rich generosity. For I testify that they
gave as much as they were able, and even beyond their ability.
Entirely on their own, they urgently pleaded with us for the privilege
of sharing in this service to the Lord's people. And they exceeded our
expectations: They gave themselves first of all to the Lord,
and then by the will of God also to us.*

2 Corinthians 8:2-5

God desires that we are generous, regardless of our
condition. Giving is a reflection of Christ, who sacrificed his
all that we may receive. Even the act of letting offenses go is
considered a gift as 'give' is the foundation of 'forgive'.

However, God expects there to be reciprocity in every
relationship.

*Our desire is not that others might be relieved while you are hard
pressed, but that there might be equality. At the present time your
plenty will supply what they need, so that in turn their plenty will
supply what you need. The goal is equality, as it is written: "The one
who gathered much did not have too much, and the one who gathered
little did not have too little."*

2 Corinthians 8:5

Therefore, it is God's desire that there be equality in
relationships. We know that those who receive much are expected
to give much. This is exemplified in Luke 12, when Jesus shared
the parable of the rich fool.

Someone in the crowd said to him, "Teacher, tell my brother to divide the inheritance with me."

Jesus replied, "Man, who appointed me a judge or an arbiter between you?" Then he said to them, "Watch out! Be on your guard against all kinds of greed; life does not consist in an abundance of possessions."

And he told them this parable: "The ground of a certain rich man yielded an abundant harvest. He thought to himself, 'What shall I do? I have no place to store my crops.'

"Then he said, 'This is what I'll do. I will tear down my barns and build bigger ones, and there I will store my surplus grain. And I'll say to myself, "You have plenty of grain laid up for many years. Take life easy; eat, drink and be merry."'

"But God said to him, 'You fool! This very night your life will be demanded from you. Then who will get what you have prepared for yourself?'

This is how it will be with whoever stores up things for themselves but is not rich toward God."

Luke 12:13-21

Our hearts are connected to our giving. God looks at the heart of man, he sees past the image, pretense, and manipulative techniques. We cannot manipulate God. He knows us, he sees us, and he has his own expectations of our behavior.

There was a couple in the Bible that was expected to sell their home and give the profits to their church group (as everyone in the church group committed to this process) that they all may live well and survive by spreading the gospel of Jesus Christ. Well, one of the couples decided that they would only give a portion of the profits instead of all of them, as they knew was their obligation. One by one, each man and wife, on separate occasions came in and lied to the leadership of their group. They each told that they received less. That day, they both died.

We can trick man, but we cannot trick the Holy Spirit. He

knows our condition. He inspects our confession. He measures our actions. He recognizes our motives. We cannot be deceived for God is not mocked.

To receive the gift of salvation that leads to eternal life, we must only confess and believe in our hearts that Christ died for us. But to gain access to an abundant life, filled with wisdom, stature, and honor, we must place God first and be about His business.

Most Gracious and Heavenly Father,

How precious are Your thoughts toward us, O God! How vast is the sum of them! (1) Every good gift and every perfect gift is from above, coming down from the Father of lights with whom there is no variation or shadow due to change. (2) Therefore, we are thankful in all circumstances, for this is God's will for us who belong to Christ Jesus. (3) Just as we received Christ Jesus as Lord, we continue to live in him, strengthened in the faith as we were taught, and overflowing with thankfulness. (4) We trust in the LORD with all our hearts, and do not lean on our own understanding. In all our ways we acknowledge him, and he will make straight our paths. (5) We will not be conformed to this world, but be transformed by the renewal of our minds, that by testing we may discern what is the will of God, what is good and acceptable and perfect. (6) And it is our prayer that our love may abound more and more, with knowledge and all discernment, so that we may approve what is excellent, and so be pure and blameless for the day of Christ. (7)

The Spirit of the Lord will rest on us—the Spirit of wisdom and of understanding, the Spirit of counsel and of might, the Spirit of the knowledge and fear of the Lord—and we will delight in the fear of the Lord. (8)

May we be dressed ready for service and keep our lamps burning, like servants waiting for their master to return from a wedding banquet, so that when he comes and knocks we can immediately open the door for him. It will be good for his servants whose master finds them watching when he comes. Truly I tell you, he will dress himself to serve, will have them recline at the table and will come and wait on us. It will be good for his servants whose master finds us ready, even if he comes in the middle of the night or toward daybreak. But understand this: If the owner of the house had known at what hour the thief was coming, he would not have let his house be broken into. We also must be ready, because the Son of Man will come at an hour when we do not expect him. (113)

In Jesus Name,
Amen

29

GIVE GOD TODAY

"Now I commit you to God and to the word of his grace, which can build you up and give you an inheritance among all those who are sanctified. I have not coveted anyone's silver or gold or clothing. You yourselves know that these hands of mine have supplied my own needs and the needs of my companions. In everything I did, I showed you that by this kind of hard work, we must help the weak, remembering the words the Lord Jesus himself said: ' It is more blessed to give than to receive.' "

Acts 20:32-35

After the crucifixion and resurrection of Jesus Christ, Paul was empowered by the Holy Spirit to preach the gospel in many nations. He was so endowed by the power of Jesus that when people would simply touch garments associated with him, they would be healed. Paul also had the ability to discern the Holy Spirit among those who followed the Lord and would simply lay hands on them to endow them with the Spirit.

Priests would even attempt to heal those sick with demons "In the name of Jesus of whom Paul preaches…" but if they were not empowered by the Holy Spirit their simple utterances were null and void. In fact, in one such instance, the demon replied to that effect and overpowered them leaving them naked and bleeding. However, their attempt to do such helped increase the word of the gospel and the power of Jesus Christ.

As Paul and his companions preached the Word of God throughout Ephesus, the tradesmen that made a great income by the sale of false gods made a great protest against the name of Jesus and those who preached it. They snatched up Paul's companions and caused a great protest locally, so much so, Paul decided not to return to Ephesus.

Instead, Paul summoned the elders of Ephesus to bid them farewell, face to face. As he communicated with them, he expressed the importance of three key factors.

1. Severe testing is necessary to accomplish the will of God.

2. Our purpose is to preach and live the gospel so that many may know God.

3. We have a responsibility to protect the body of Christ, which Christ bought with his own blood.

Paul realized that as a true disciple of Christ, a "good life" was not defined by what society deemed good, but more so by what God labels as "good." By society's definition, success is measured by outward achievements: a good job, money, power, and beauty. God looks at the heart. His measurements include integrity, commitment, humility, and grace.

When we live a life that is committed to giving God what he desires today, we in turn are blessing someone with the gift of God today.

To receive the gift of salvation that leads to eternal life, we must only confess and believe in our hearts that Christ died for us. But to gain access to an abundant life, filled with wisdom, stature, and honor, we must place God first and be about His business.

Most Gracious and Heavenly Father,

How precious are Your thoughts toward us, O God! How vast is the sum of them! (1) Every good gift and every perfect gift is from above, coming down from the Father of lights with whom there is no variation or shadow due to change. (2) Therefore, we are thankful in all circumstances, for this is God's will for us who belong to Christ Jesus. (3) Just as we received Christ Jesus as Lord, we continue to live in him, strengthened in the faith as we were taught, and overflowing with thankfulness. (4) We trust in the LORD with all our hearts, and do not lean on our own understanding. In all our ways we acknowledge him, and he will make straight our paths. (5) We will not be conformed to this world, but be transformed by the renewal of our minds, that by testing we may discern what is the will of God, what is good and acceptable and perfect. (6) And it is our prayer that our love may abound more and more, with knowledge and all discernment, so that we may approve what is excellent, and so be pure and blameless for the day of Christ. (7)

The Spirit of the Lord will rest on us—the Spirit of wisdom and of understanding, the Spirit of counsel and of might, the Spirit of the knowledge and fear of the Lord—and we will delight in the fear of the Lord. (8)

God is not human, that he should lie, not a human being, that he should change his mind. Does he speak and then not act? Does he promise and not fulfill? (114) The Lord is not slow in keeping his promise, as some understand slowness. Instead he is patient with you, not wanting anyone to perish, but everyone to come to repentance. (115) God's way is perfect: The LORD's word is flawless; he shields all who take refuge in him. (116) The LORD is gracious and righteous; our God is full of compassion. (117) No temptation has overtaken you except what is common to mankind. And God is faithful; he will not let you be tempted beyond what you can bear. But when you are tempted, he will also provide a way out so that you can endure it. (118)

In Jesus Name,
Amen

30

STRETCH

Lord our God, you answered them; you were to Israel a forgiving God, though you punished their misdeeds. Exalt the Lord our God and worship at his holy mountain, for the Lord our God is holy.

Psalm 99:8-9

We are not holy people by default. It requires an intentional shift in our thinking and decision-making in order for us to become holy people. Holiness walks hand-in-hand with humility, forgiveness, mercy and grace.

Anger does not produce holiness, but anger is resilient in its pursuit of justice, equality, and respect. People often mistake a light shined on injustice as a byproduct of pride. When one group of people sees angry and hurt people protesting in the streets that group of people are angered, but those people are often begging for justice, equality, and respect of life.

So how do we receive justice while being holy?

We let God fight the battle. Which I can attest is easier said then done.

Dearly beloved, avenge not yourselves, but rather give place unto wrath: for it is written, Vengeance is mine; I will repay, saith the Lord. Therefore if thine enemy hunger, feed him; if he thirst, give him drink: for in so doing thou shalt heap coals of fire on his head.

Romans 12:19-21

People will take your kindness as a weakness. They will use you as a comfortable place to rest from their hard work and their efforts, that they may take advantage of your willingness to obey God. There is no doubt that this will cause anger and resentment. The anger and resentment will not be directed at them forever, at some point, you will find yourself angry with God. You will be angry because you have committed your life to him and his way and you feel defenseless and without a path of recourse for justice. You will feel like Joseph serving time for a crime he was accused of yet didn't commit. Or like David, a young king on the rise, sought by a man who lost his reign on leadership and destroyed his own relationship wth God.

David and Joseph passed their tests and became great men. Samson, the strongest man in the world was full of might and fury but could not resist his anger and quest for justice. His anger and quest for love and acceptance left him without sound decision-making and he was eventually stripped of his power and blinded before killing more than 3,000 of his enemies and losing his own life in the process.

Choosing to live a life that is pleasing to God is not always comfortable. There are often more dark seasons than seasons of laughter, love, and happiness. This is so that we may live an eternal life without tears or injustice. In this world, we are on a battlefield against forces of darkness that are trying to quiet and dim our light. But God is love. We are to walk in love, no matter the cost and trust God to fight every battle we face. Victory is on the other side.

To receive the gift of salvation that leads to eternal life, we must only confess and believe in our hearts that Christ died for us. But to gain access to an abundant life, filled with wisdom, stature, and honor, we must place God first and be about His business.

Most Gracious and Heavenly Father,

How precious are Your thoughts toward us, O God! How vast is the sum of them! (1) Every good gift and every perfect gift is from above, coming down from the Father of lights with whom there is no variation or shadow due to change. (2) Therefore, we are thankful in all circumstances, for this is God's will for us who belong to Christ Jesus. (3) Just as we received Christ Jesus as Lord, we continue to live in him, strengthened in the faith as we were taught, and overflowing with thankfulness. (4) We trust in the LORD with all our hearts, and do not lean on our own understanding. In all our ways we acknowledge him, and he will make straight our paths. (5) We will not be conformed to this world, but be transformed by the renewal of our minds, that by testing we may discern what is the will of God, what is good and acceptable and perfect. (6) And it is our prayer that our love may abound more and more, with knowledge and all discernment, so that we may approve what is excellent, and so be pure and blameless for the day of Christ. (7)

The Spirit of the Lord will rest on us—the Spirit of wisdom and of understanding, the Spirit of counsel and of might, the Spirit of the knowledge and fear of the Lord—and we will delight in the fear of the Lord. (8)

Be not overcome of evil, but overcome evil with good. (119)

In Jesus Name,
Amen

31

BY FAITH

Against all hope, Abraham in hope believed and so became the father of many nations, just as it had been said to him, "So shall your offspring be." Without weakening in his faith, he faced the fact that his body was as good as dead—since he was about a hundred years old—and that Sarah's womb was also dead. Yet he did not waver through unbelief regarding the promise of God, but was strengthened in his faith and gave glory to God, being fully persuaded that God had power to do what he had promised. This is why "it was credited to him as righteousness."

Romans 4:18-22

It is our responsibility to always stay in the will of God. This can only be possible by faith. Time and opportunity will slip through our hands and the promise God made to us can seem like it will never come to pass. But God is faithful. He will do as he promised. If we can just wait on him.

The joy of the Lord is our strength.

The wicked plot against the righteous and gnash their teeth at them; but the Lord laughs at the wicked, for he knows their day is coming. The wicked draw the sword and bend the bow to bring down the poor and needy, to slay those whose ways are upright. But their swords will pierce their own hearts, and their bows will be broken. Better the little that the righteous have than the wealth of many wicked; for the power of the wicked will be broken, but the Lord upholds the righteous.

Psalm 37:12-15

Our faith will carry us through. Only God can declare us righteous regardless of circumstance. God is our shield and our great reward. God is our waymaker.

Our dedication must remain to God and not to man, for if we fail or falter, God will pick us up. Man will shun us and throw us away, but God is merciful and forgiving, his love endures forever.

To receive the gift of salvation that leads to eternal life, we must only confess and believe in our hearts that Christ died for us. But to gain access to an abundant life, filled with wisdom, stature, and honor, we must place God first and be about His business.

Most Gracious and Heavenly Father,

How precious are Your thoughts toward us, O God! How vast is the sum of them! (1) Every good gift and every perfect gift is from above, coming down from the Father of lights with whom there is no variation or shadow due to change. (2) Therefore, we are thankful in all circumstances, for this is God's will for us who belong to Christ Jesus. (3) Just as we received Christ Jesus as Lord, we continue to live in him, strengthened in the faith as we were taught, and overflowing with thankfulness. (4) We trust in the LORD with all our hearts, and do not lean on our own understanding. In all our ways we acknowledge him, and he will make straight our paths. (5) We will not be conformed to this world, but be transformed by the renewal of our minds, that by testing we may discern what is the will of God, what is good and acceptable and perfect. (6) And it is our prayer that our love may abound more and more, with knowledge and all discernment, so that we may approve what is excellent, and so be pure and blameless for the day of Christ. (7)

The Spirit of the Lord will rest on us—the Spirit of wisdom and of understanding, the Spirit of counsel and of might, the Spirit of the knowledge and fear of the Lord—and we will delight in the fear of the Lord. (8)

But the Lord is faithful. He will establish us and guard us against the evil one. (120) The steadfast love of the LORD never ceases; his mercies never come to an end; they are new every morning; great is your faithfulness. (121) Jesus Christ is the same yesterday and today and forever. (122) The saying is trustworthy, for: If we have died with him, we will also live with him; if we endure, we will also reign with him; if we deny him, he also will deny us; if we are faithless, he remains faithful—for he cannot deny himself. (123) Grace to each of us and peace from him who is and who was and who is to come, and from the seven spirits who are before his throne, and from Jesus Christ the faithful witness, the firstborn of the dead, and the ruler of kings on earth. To him who loves us and has freed us from our sins by his blood (124)

In Jesus Name,
Amen

CITATIONS

1. Psalm 139:7
2. James 1:17
3. I Thessalonians 5:18
4. Colossians 2:6
5. Proverbs 3:5-6
6. Romans 12:2
7. Phillipians 1:9-10
8. Isaiah 11:2-3
9. Luke 11:33-38
10. I Corinthians 12:12,14
11. John 16:13
12. Jeremiah 17:7
13. 2 Peter 3:18
14. I Chronicles 4:10
15. Ephesians 4:31
16. James 1:19-20
17. Proverbs 29:11
18. Proverbs 19:11
19. Psalm 37:8-9
20. Psalm 7:10-11
21. Proverbs 7:14-17
22. Psalm 73:25-26
23. 2 Corinthians 12:9
24. Psalm 62:7
25. I Corinthians 6:17
26. John 15:4-5
27. I Corinthians 2:14
28. James 3:17
29. Philippians 1:9-10
30. I Kings 3:9
31. Matthew 10:16
37. https://knowledge.autodesk.com: Types of Reflection
38. Colossians 2:6
39. Romans 8:4
40. I John 4:17
41. Romans 14:8
42. I Thessalonians 5:23
43. Ephesians 5:6-7
44. I John 4:1
45. Matthew 7:6
46. Romans 11:33-36
47. I John 5:14
48. Hebrews 11:1

49. James 5:16
50. I Timothy 2:1-2
51. Hebrews 11:6
52. Psalm 44:4-8
53. Matthew 6:9-13
54. Deuteronomy 9:29
55. 2 Kings 13:4-5
56. Psalm 14:4-5
57. Psalm 112
58. 2 Corinthians 10:5
59. Revelation 14:12
60. 2 John 1:6
61. Isaiah 30:21
62. Jeremiah 29:11
63. I Corinthians 1:25
64. Psalm 37:23
65. Habakkuk 2:3
66. Hebrews 12:2
67. Isaiah 58:9b - 12
68. Psalm 22:3
69. Matthew 18:20
70. Revelations 5:8
71. 2 Chronicles 16:9a
72. Psalm 71:22-24
73. Galatians 6:7-10
74. John 15:9-17
75. I Peter 4:7-11
76. Exodus 15:11
77. I Chronicles 29:11
78. Psalm 19:1
79. Psalm 24:7-8
80. Psalm 104:31-32
81. Psalm 115:1
82. 2 Chronicles 20:17
83. Deuteronomy 3:22
84. Isaiah 54:17
85. Isaiah 25:1
86. Psalm 150:6
87. John 4:24
88. Psalm 81:15-16
89. Ecclesiastes 11:6
90. Galatians 6:8
91. Luke 8:15
92. Genesis 26:12
93. 2 Corinthians 9:6 - 15
94. Psalm 27:1
95. Romans 8:31-32
96. Proverbs 28:1
97. Hebrews 4:16
98. 2 Corinthians 3:12

99. Ephesians 1:5
100. John 1:12-13
101. Romans 8:14-17
102. Psalm 23:4
103. John 14:17
104. Psalm 56:3-4
105. Ephesians 6:10
106. I Corinthians 2:3
107. Deuteronomy 20:1
108. Romans 8:28
109. Psalm 46:10
110. Philippians 3:13-14
111. Ephesians 3:21-21
112. Psalm 46
113. Luke 12:35-40
114. Numbers 23:19
115. 2 Peter 3:9
116. Psalm 18:30
117. Psalm 116:5
118. I Corinthians 10:13
119. Romans 12:21
120. 2 Thessalonians 3:3
121. Lamentations 3:22-23
122. Hebrews 13:8
123. 2 Timothy 2:11-13
124. Revelation 1:4-5

About the Author

At the age of 9, Stephanie was molested by a friend of my family. In high school, she held the hand of a friend as he died from a fatal gun shot wound... As an adult, she was the victim of a violent acquaintance rape. Subsequently, she struggled with personal demons. But when she sought the Lord and his Word, her life was forever changed.

Give God ALL the Glory!

He is and will always be the head of my life. He is my joy, my strength, my everything. My constant prayer is to be a perfect conduit of his message and love.

stephanie d. moore

Stephanie was born in Muskogee, Oklahoma. She graduated from Putnam City North High School in 1994. She was married for 16 years. She is the mother of 3 beautiful daughters, and has a grandson named Levi. She graduated with her Associates in Technology, a Bachelor of Arts in Communications, and a Master of Arts in Communication with an emphasis in Political Communication.

She holds several design and technology certifications and has won numerous awards in that area. Stephanie has worked in television, print and web media for more than 18 years.

She is the owner of Moore Marketing and Communications. Her company offers strategic marketing and communication plans, media purchases, public relations, writing services, print services, graphic design and web design. Stephanie has also served as a poltical consultant for Governor, Lt. Governor, State Representative, Mayoral and City Council candidates.

Stephanie has created and sponsored teen etiquette and leadership programs for young ladies and young men. The program for young ladies is called, She's a BOSSE (A Beautiful Oasis of Success, Style and Elegance) and the young man's program is called Grindaholix: Young Men on the Rise.

To date, Stephanie has authored 34 books, 18 of which are daily devotionals. To learn more, visit mooretoread.com.